LIVE BIG

MOMENTUM
MAKER

LIVE BIG 90-DAY MOMENTUM MAKER

LiveBigWithStacey.com

Designed by Esther Moody
Edited by Lori Lynn Enterprises
Published by Transcendent Publishing | TranscendentPublishing.com

ISBN: 979-8-9922207-1-1

Printed in the United States of America

WELCOME

Welcome to the LIVE BIG *90-Day Momentum Maker*! This isn't just any journal or planner—it's your personal roadmap to building a life and business that aligns with your deepest vision and biggest dreams. This is the exact system I used to break free from the ordinary and live a BIG life that ignites my soul.

Together with the *LIVE BIG* book, this tool is here to help you tackle each day with clarity, focus, and intention, turning your target outcomes into tangible results. (By the way, if you don't have a copy of the LIVE BIG book, you can head over to **LiveBigWithStacey.com/book** or scan the QR code below to grab your copy.)

LiveBigWithStacey.com/book

Over the next 90 days, you'll be creating powerful momentum—momentum that drives your growth and keeps you steadily moving toward the life you're meant to live.

WHY MOMENTUM?

Momentum is the game-changer between dreaming and achieving. Every day you show up for yourself with intention, you're planting seeds in your Garden of Dreams (don't miss Chapters 3 and 4 in the *LIVE BIG* book!), building habits and routines that nurture a force too powerful to ignore.

Momentum is what transforms your dreams into reality. It's that forward-moving energy born from consistent action, each step building on the last. And here's the scoop: those who achieve BIG results aren't the ones who sprint and stop; they're the ones who show up every day, nurturing their dreams and tending to their growth. Momentum builds resilience, and resilience is your secret weapon for turning your dreams into reality.

WHY 90 DAYS?

Growth happens gradually, and seeing progress in the thick of the daily grind isn't always easy. By focusing on 90-day periods, you'll gain the chance to look back each quarter, celebrate your wins, and set your sights even higher.

Every 90 days, you'll see that you're not just dreaming—you're planting, cultivating, and building something real. Your Garden of Dreams will flourish as you move through each quarter, and you'll witness the impact of your dedication.

This *90-Day Momentum Maker* will guide you in mastering the art of consistency. Every day, you'll map out priorities, set intentions, and reflect on the incredible life and business you're building.

But this isn't only about productivity—it's about grounding yourself in the bigger picture. Journaling and planning are more than simple tools; they're a daily practice that connects you with your vision, building a mindset that empowers you every step of the way.

And because I wanted this to be your go-to companion anywhere you go, I kept it portable. Slip it into your purse, bag, or suitcase—whether you're at home, on the go, or in the middle of a packed day, this little powerhouse will be right there to help you stay focused, aligned, and inspired.

BOSS² UP, SHOW UP, AND STEP UP

Here's my challenge for you …

Make these 90 days count. Lean into the process, water your Garden of Dreams with daily action, and watch as your biggest visions take root and flourish. This is your moment to Boss² Up your business, Show Up for yourself, and Step Up into your most productive, resilient, and beautiful version of you.

It's your time to LIVE BIG, every single day.

Now, let's dive in!

90-DAY DREAM SEEDS

Your Dream Seeds are the heart of your *90-Day Momentum Maker*—the powerful outcomes you want to bring to life. Over the next 90 days, you're not just "setting goals," you're creating the building blocks for the life and business you've envisioned. Let's dive in and plant those Dream Seeds with clarity and intention.

1. What are your top 1 to 3 Dream Seeds—the specific target outcomes you're determined to bring to life over the next 90 days? Think BIG, be specific, and make it measurable! *(Examples: "Reduce expenses by 10%," "Enroll 50 new clients," "Launch my online course.")*

2. Why are these Dream Seeds important to you? What will achieving these mean for your life and your future? This is your "why" that will fuel your commitment.

3. Are these Dream Seeds within your control? Make sure each one is something you can directly influence—outcomes that depend on *your* actions, not on anyone else's decisions.

4. How do these Dream Seeds fit into your bigger vision for the next 12 months? Picture the life you're designing. How will these target outcomes help you bring that vision closer to reality?

Tip: If you haven't already, dive into Chapters 3 and 4 of *LIVE BIG* to refine your vision and learn how to plant Dream Seeds that will thrive. As you work through this *90-Day Momentum Maker*, remember that your daily actions should always align with these Dream Seeds. And with each action you take, you're intentionally shaping the future you desire.

DAILY PLANNER

Are you ready to build unstoppable momentum, reach your target outcomes, and live your life with purpose? This workbook will equip you with the tools to turn your dreams into action and make daily progress toward the life you envision.

So, what's in store? Each page is thoughtfully designed to keep you focused on what matters most:

1. Gratitude. You'll start your day by listing three things or people you're grateful for and *why* you're grateful for them. Cultivating gratitude fuels a positive mindset, setting you up for success.

2. Daily Commitments. You'll outline the top three tasks you're committing to today. These aren't just items on a to-do list—they're the purposeful actions that will nurture and grow your Dream Seeds.

3. Learning. You'll be intentional about what you're learning on a daily basis, whether it's a new skill, an insight from a conversation, or a piece of wisdom. This habit keeps you growth-oriented and open to the valuable lessons around you.

4. Serving Others. You'll think about how you'll serve others, whether it's through kindness, mentorship, or your work. This focus reminds you that success is not just about personal gains but also about positively impacting others.

5. Self-Care. You'll also be intentional about how you're showing up for yourself day by day. Success requires that you invest in your own well-being, and you'll make sure to prioritize self-care as part of your routine.

6. Visualization. You'll spend a few moments with a powerful visualization activity, focusing your mind and energy. Each day, you'll frame what success feels and looks like, fueling your drive and confidence with a clear vision.

7. Affirmations. On the daily, you'll write down at least one positive affirmation. Say it aloud and give it power—speak it with energy, belief, and emotion. I'll also be providing you with a **Daily Dose of Awesome**, a simple yet powerful way to reinforce a positive mindset.

8. Journaling. In addition to daily planning, this journal includes space for deeper reflection. Capture your thoughts, insights, and breakthroughs to stay connected to your journey. For extra guidance, you can download journal prompts at livebigwithstacey.com/resources.

Each section is designed to help you stay focused, consistent, and intentional as you take daily steps toward your vision. This is your 90-day commitment to growth, gratitude, and forward motion. Let every practice here remind you of your purpose, fuel your progress, and empower you to LIVE BIG—starting now.

CREATE YOUR OWN ROUTINE

There's no "right" or "wrong" way to fill out the pages of your *90-Day Momentum Maker*. You might find that taking 20 minutes each morning to plan your day and returning in the evening to journal works best for you. Or, you may prefer to plan for the following day in the afternoon and journal in the morning.

The key is to explore what feels natural and effective, then create a routine you can stick with. This is *your* journey—embrace a rhythm that fuels your momentum and aligns with how you show up best.

Are you ready to dive in? Let's build momentum, one day at a time!

3 Things/People I'm Grateful for Today and why you're grateful for them

ACTION STEP: If you've listed people here, send them a note to tell them.

1.

2.

3.

"To Do's" I'm Committing to Accomplish Today

ACTION STEP: Time block your to-do's in your calendar.

1.

2.

3.

What Am I Learning Today?	How Am I Serving Others Today?

How Am I Showing Up for Myself Today?

VISUALIZATION

Imagine yourself moving through today with calm confidence. Feel a sense of ease as you tackle each task. Imagine the feeling of clarity and assurance in every decision. *What would it feel like to trust yourself completely? Let this sensation settle into your body, guiding you through your day.*

AFFIRMATION

Write at least one positive affirmation that resonates with you today and say it out loud.

DAILY DOSE OF AWESOME

I am calm, confident, and capable in all that I do.

Say this affirmation aloud at least seven times and use different inflection points each time.

JOURNAL

Feeling stuck about what to write about today and need some inspiration?
Scan this QR code:

3 Things/People I'm Grateful for Today and why you're grateful for them
ACTION STEP: If you've listed people here, send them a note to tell them.

1.

2.

3.

"To Do's" I'm Committing to Accomplish Today
ACTION STEP: Time block your to-do's in your calendar.

1.

2.

3.

What Am I Learning Today?   ## How Am I Serving Others Today?

How Am I Showing Up for Myself Today?

VISUALIZATION

Picture yourself facing a challenge today and responding with resilience and grace. See yourself meeting the challenge with strength and resourcefulness. How does it feel to know you have everything within you to overcome obstacles? *Anchor this feeling within you as a reminder of your inner power.*

DAILY DOSE OF AWESOME
I have the resilience and strength to overcome any challenge.
Say this affirmation aloud at least seven times and use different inflection points each time.

AFFIRMATION

Write at least one positive affirmation that resonates with you today and say it out loud.

JOURNAL

Feeling stuck about what to write about today and need some inspiration?
Scan this QR code:

3 Things/People I'm Grateful for Today and why you're grateful for them
ACTION STEP: If you've listed people here, send them a note to tell them.

1.

2.

3.

"To Do's" I'm Committing to Accomplish Today
ACTION STEP: Time block your to-do's in your calendar.

1.

2.

3.

What Am I Learning Today?	How Am I Serving Others Today?

How Am I Showing Up for Myself Today?

VISUALIZATION

Visualize sharing your dreams with a potential client or partner. Imagine the excitement in their eyes as they connect with your passion. Feel the pride in expressing your purpose with clarity. *Let this experience boost your confidence as you step into new conversations today.*

DAILY DOSE OF AWESOME

My vision is powerful, and
I share it with pride.

Say this affirmation aloud at least seven times and
use different inflection points each time.

AFFIRMATION

Write at least one positive affirmation that
resonates with you today and say it out loud.

JOURNAL

3 Things/People I'm Grateful for Today and why you're grateful for them
ACTION STEP: If you've listed people here, send them a note to tell them.

1.

2.

3.

"To Do's" I'm Committing to Accomplish Today
ACTION STEP: Time block your to-do's in your calendar.

1.

2.

3.

What Am I Learning Today?   ## How Am I Serving Others Today?

How Am I Showing Up for Myself Today?

VISUALIZATION

See yourself looking at your task list, feeling focused and fully in control. Imagine the satisfaction of prioritizing with ease, knowing exactly what needs to be done. Breathe in the feeling of purpose and dedication—*let it energize you as you set your day's intentions.*

AFFIRMATION
Write at least one positive affirmation that resonates with you today and say it out loud.

DAILY DOSE OF AWESOME
I am focused and fully in control of my day.
Say this affirmation aloud at least seven times and use different inflection points each time.

JOURNAL

Feeling stuck about what to write about today and need some inspiration?
Scan this QR code:

3 Things/People I'm Grateful for Today and why you're grateful for them
ACTION STEP: If you've listed people here, send them a note to tell them.

1. ....

2. ....

3. ....

"To Do's" I'm Committing to Accomplish Today
ACTION STEP: Time block your to-do's in your calendar.

1. ....

2. ....

3. ....

What Am I Learning Today?

....

....

....

How Am I Serving Others Today?

....

....

....

How Am I Showing Up for Myself Today?

....

....

VISUALIZATION

Picture yourself as a powerful leader, fully in control, making empowered decisions. Visualize your team, friends, and family looking to you with trust and respect. How does it feel to be seen as a leader? *Let this sense of purpose and capability carry you through today.*

DAILY DOSE OF AWESOME
I am a strong leader who is trusted and respected.
Say this affirmation aloud at least seven times and use different inflection points each time.

AFFIRMATION
Write at least one positive affirmation that resonates with you today and say it out loud.

....

....

....

....

JOURNAL

3 Things/People I'm Grateful for Today and why you're grateful for them
ACTION STEP: If you've listed people here, send them a note to tell them.

1.

2.

3.

"To Do's" I'm Committing to Accomplish Today
ACTION STEP: Time block your to-do's in your calendar.

1.

2.

3.

What Am I Learning Today?

How Am I Serving Others Today?

How Am I Showing Up for Myself Today?

VISUALIZATION

Recall a recent challenge and visualize how you successfully moved past it. Feel the growth and strength that came from overcoming it. Remind yourself of the lessons learned and the resilience gained. *This is your proof that you can handle whatever comes your way.*

DAILY DOSE OF AWESOME
Every challenge I face
strengthens and grows me.
Say this affirmation aloud at least seven times and use different inflection points each time.

AFFIRMATION
Write at least one positive affirmation that resonates with you today and say it out loud.

JOURNAL

3 Things/People I'm Grateful for Today and why you're grateful for them
ACTION STEP: If you've listed people here, send them a note to tell them.

1.

2.

3.

"To Do's" I'm Committing to Accomplish Today
ACTION STEP: Time block your to-do's in your calendar.

1.

2.

3.

What Am I Learning Today?	How Am I Serving Others Today?

How Am I Showing Up for Myself Today?

VISUALIZATION

Imagine receiving recognition for your hard work—feel the pride and appreciation. Picture this acknowledgment from a client, friend, or family member, and let it fill you with gratitude. *Allow yourself to bask in the feeling of being valued and respected.*

AFFIRMATION

Write at least one positive affirmation that resonates with you today and say it out loud.

DAILY DOSE OF AWESOME

I am valued and appreciated for my hard work.

Say this affirmation aloud at least seven times and use different inflection points each time.

JOURNAL

Feeling stuck about what to write about today and need some inspiration?
Scan this QR code:

WEEKLY PROGRESS CELEBRATION:
WEED PATROL & PROGRESS TRACKING

Congratulations on another week of growing your Dream Seeds! This **Weekly Progress Celebration** is your time to reflect on all you've accomplished, identify any challenges, and keep your progress on track. Set aside 30 minutes to do a little "weed patrol" and celebrate your wins.

1. Weed Patrol

Take a moment to check in with yourself. **Are there any "weeds" (negative thoughts, self-doubt, or roadblocks) that have sprouted up this week?** Write down anything that has held you back or weighed on you.

Examples of weeds could be:
+ Doubts about your capabilities
+ Negative self-talk
+ Unanticipated obstacles

How will you "nip them in the bud" and keep moving forward? Describe a pro-active step or mindset shift to tackle these weeds.

2. Action Review

Reflect on the actions you took during this past week. **Did these actions effectively nurture your Dream Seeds and target outcomes?**

+ What daily actions worked well in nurturing your goals?
+ Were there any actions that felt unproductive or off-track?

List a few adjustments you could make for next week to keep your actions aligned with your vision.

3. Initiative Check

Review the initiatives in your Watering Cans. **Are you on track to achieve each one?** Take a quick look at your key focus areas and consider any adjustments needed.

Which initiatives are moving along well?

Are there any that need a bit more attention or a different approach?

Note any tweaks or new strategies to strengthen your progress next week.

_____

_____

_____

_____

4. Celebrate Success!

Time to celebrate! **What successes or progress can you acknowledge this week?** Whether big or small, every step forward counts. Take a moment to recognize what you've accomplished, and feel proud of yourself for showing up.

+ What are you most proud of this week?
+ How can you reward yourself or simply honor your efforts?

Remember, progress isn't always about huge leaps—it's about steady, consistent steps forward. Give yourself credit for every victory.

_____

_____

_____

_____

3 Things/People I'm Grateful for Today and why you're grateful for them
ACTION STEP: If you've listed people here, send them a note to tell them.

1.

2.

3.

"To Do's" I'm Committing to Accomplish Today
ACTION STEP: Time block your to-do's in your calendar.

1.

2.

3.

What Am I Learning Today?

How Am I Serving Others Today?

How Am I Showing Up for Myself Today?

VISUALIZATION
Visualize giving yourself grace to learn from mistakes instead of dwelling on them. Imagine letting go of self-criticism and replacing it with self-compassion. How does it feel to embrace progress over perfection? *Carry this sense of self-kindness as you move forward.*

AFFIRMATION
Write at least one positive affirmation that resonates with you today and say it out loud.

DAILY DOSE OF AWESOME
I give myself grace and celebrate progress over perfection.
Say this affirmation aloud at least seven times and use different inflection points each time.

JOURNAL

3 Things/People I'm Grateful for Today and why you're grateful for them
ACTION STEP: If you've listed people here, send them a note to tell them.

1.

2.

3.

"To Do's" I'm Committing to Accomplish Today
ACTION STEP: Time block your to-do's in your calendar.

1.

2.

3.

What Am I Learning Today?	How Am I Serving Others Today?

How Am I Showing Up for Myself Today?

VISUALIZATION
See your calendar balanced with dedicated time for work, family, and self-care. Imagine the peace and fulfillment that comes from honoring each area of your life. *Feel the satisfaction of balance, knowing you're showing up fully for what matters most.*

AFFIRMATION
Write at least one positive affirmation that resonates with you today and say it out loud.

DAILY DOSE OF AWESOME
I create balance in my life
with purpose and ease.
Say this affirmation aloud at least seven times and use different inflection points each time.

JOURNAL

Feeling stuck about what to write about today and need some inspiration?
Scan this QR code:

3 Things/People I'm Grateful for Today and why you're grateful for them

ACTION STEP: If you've listed people here, send them a note to tell them.

1.

2.

3.

"To Do's" I'm Committing to Accomplish Today

ACTION STEP: Time block your to-do's in your calendar.

1.

2.

3.

What Am I Learning Today?

How Am I Serving Others Today?

How Am I Showing Up for Myself Today?

VISUALIZATION

Picture yourself in a moment today where you feel truly connected to your purpose. Imagine the clarity, excitement, and passion that flows when you're aligned with what you love. *Let this feeling sink in, grounding you in why you do what you do.*

AFFIRMATION

Write at least one positive affirmation that resonates with you today and say it out loud.

DAILY DOSE OF AWESOME

I am fully connected to my purpose and passion.

Say this affirmation aloud at least seven times and use different inflection points each time.

JOURNAL

Feeling stuck about what to write about today and need some inspiration?
Scan this QR code:

3 Things/People I'm Grateful for Today and why you're grateful for them
ACTION STEP: If you've listed people here, send them a note to tell them.

1.

2.

3.

"To Do's" I'm Committing to Accomplish Today
ACTION STEP: Time block your to-do's in your calendar.

1.

2.

3.

What Am I Learning Today?   ## How Am I Serving Others Today?

How Am I Showing Up for Myself Today?

VISUALIZATION
Picture yourself confidently sharing an idea with someone important. Feel the courage and trust in your voice as you speak. *Embrace the sense of self-assurance that comes from owning your worth and ideas.*

AFFIRMATION
Write at least one positive affirmation that resonates with you today and say it out loud.

DAILY DOSE OF AWESOME
I am courageous and trust myself completely.
Say this affirmation aloud at least seven times and use different inflection points each time.

JOURNAL

Feeling stuck about what to write about today and need some inspiration? Scan this QR code:

3 Things/People I'm Grateful for Today and why you're grateful for them
ACTION STEP: If you've listed people here, send them a note to tell them.

1.

2.

3.

"To Do's" I'm Committing to Accomplish Today
ACTION STEP: Time block your to-do's in your calendar.

1.

2.

3.

What Am I Learning Today?   ## How Am I Serving Others Today?

How Am I Showing Up for Myself Today?

VISUALIZATION
Visualize yourself ending today with a sense of accomplishment and peace. Imagine looking back at the day, proud of what you've achieved. *Feel the deep satisfaction of progress and let it encourage you for tomorrow.*

AFFIRMATION
Write at least one positive affirmation that resonates with you today and say it out loud.

DAILY DOSE OF AWESOME
I am proud of what I am achieving today.
Say this affirmation aloud at least seven times and use different inflection points each time.

JOURNAL

3 Things/People I'm Grateful for Today and why you're grateful for them
ACTION STEP: If you've listed people here, send them a note to tell them.

1.

2.

3.

"To Do's" I'm Committing to Accomplish Today
ACTION STEP: Time block your to-do's in your calendar.

1.

2.

3.

What Am I Learning Today?

How Am I Serving Others Today?

How Am I Showing Up for Myself Today?

VISUALIZATION
See yourself fully present during family time, without distractions. Feel the warmth of being completely connected with your loved ones. *Let this sense of connection ground you and recharge your spirit.*

AFFIRMATION
Write at least one positive affirmation that resonates with you today and say it out loud.

DAILY DOSE OF AWESOME
I am present and create meaningful memories with my loved ones.
Say this affirmation aloud at least seven times and use different inflection points each time.

JOURNAL

Feeling stuck about what to write about today and need some inspiration?
Scan this QR code:

3 Things/People I'm Grateful for Today and why you're grateful for them
ACTION STEP: If you've listed people here, send them a note to tell them.

1.

2.

3.

"To Do's" I'm Committing to Accomplish Today
ACTION STEP: Time block your to-do's in your calendar.

1.

2.

3.

What Am I Learning Today?

How Am I Serving Others Today?

How Am I Showing Up for Myself Today?

VISUALIZATION
Imagine responding calmly to a stressful situation today. See yourself managing it with poise and strength. *Embrace the confidence that comes from staying centered, regardless of what comes your way.*

AFFIRMATION
Write at least one positive affirmation that resonates with you today and say it out loud.

DAILY DOSE OF AWESOME
I am calm, steady, and centered, no matter what.
Say this affirmation aloud at least seven times and use different inflection points each time.

JOURNAL

Feeling stuck about what to write about today and need some inspiration? Scan this QR code:

WEEKLY PROGRESS CELEBRATION:
WEED PATROL & PROGRESS TRACKING

Congratulations on another week of growing your Dream Seeds! This **Weekly Progress Celebration** is your time to reflect on all you've accomplished, identify any challenges, and keep your progress on track. Set aside 30 minutes to do a little "weed patrol" and celebrate your wins.

1. Weed Patrol

Take a moment to check in with yourself. **Are there any "weeds" (negative thoughts, self-doubt, or roadblocks) that have sprouted up this week?** Write down anything that has held you back or weighed on you.

Examples of weeds could be:
+ Doubts about your capabilities
+ Negative self-talk
+ Unanticipated obstacles

How will you "nip them in the bud" and keep moving forward? Describe a proactive step or mindset shift to tackle these weeds.

_____

_____

_____

_____

2. Action Review

Reflect on the actions you took during this past week. **Did these actions effectively nurture your Dream Seeds and target outcomes?**

+ What daily actions worked well in nurturing your goals?
+ Were there any actions that felt unproductive or off-track?

List a few adjustments you could make for next week to keep your actions aligned with your vision.

_____

_____

_____

3. Initiative Check

Review the initiatives in your Watering Cans. **Are you on track to achieve each one?** Take a quick look at your key focus areas and consider any adjustments needed.

Which initiatives are moving along well?

Are there any that need a bit more attention or a different approach?

Note any tweaks or new strategies to strengthen your progress next week.

_____

_____

_____

_____

_____

4. Celebrate Success!

Time to celebrate! **What successes or progress can you acknowledge this week?** Whether big or small, every step forward counts. Take a moment to recognize what you've accomplished, and feel proud of yourself for showing up.

- What are you most proud of this week?
- How can you reward yourself or simply honor your efforts?

Remember, progress isn't always about huge leaps—it's about steady, consistent steps forward. Give yourself credit for every victory.

_____

_____

_____

_____

_____

3 Things/People I'm Grateful for Today and why you're grateful for them
ACTION STEP: If you've listed people here, send them a note to tell them.

1. ....

2. ....

3. ....

"To Do's" I'm Committing to Accomplish Today
ACTION STEP: Time block your to-do's in your calendar.

1. ....

2. ....

3. ....

What Am I Learning Today? | How Am I Serving Others Today?

How Am I Showing Up for Myself Today?

VISUALIZATION
Visualize yourself taking bold action on a decision you've been hesitant about. Picture yourself feeling confident and decisive. Embrace the freedom that comes from trusting your instincts.

AFFIRMATION
Write at least one positive affirmation that resonates with you today and say it out loud.

DAILY DOSE OF AWESOME
I take bold action and
trust my instincts.
Say this affirmation aloud at least seven times and use different inflection points each time.

JOURNAL

Feeling stuck about what to write about today and need some inspiration?
Scan this QR code:

3 Things/People I'm Grateful for Today and why you're grateful for them
ACTION STEP: If you've listed people here, send them a note to tell them.

1.

2.

3.

"To Do's" I'm Committing to Accomplish Today
ACTION STEP: Time block your to-do's in your calendar.

1.

2.

3.

What Am I Learning Today?

How Am I Serving Others Today?

How Am I Showing Up for Myself Today?

VISUALIZATION
See yourself advocating confidently for your ideas in a meeting. Imagine the positive response and respect from others. *Let the feeling of being valued strengthen your belief in yourself.*

AFFIRMATION
Write at least one positive affirmation that resonates with you today and say it out loud.

DAILY DOSE OF AWESOME
My ideas are worthy, and I share them confidently.
Say this affirmation aloud at least seven times and use different inflection points each time.

JOURNAL

3 Things/People I'm Grateful for Today and why you're grateful for them
ACTION STEP: If you've listed people here, send them a note to tell them.

1.

2.

3.

"To Do's" I'm Committing to Accomplish Today
ACTION STEP: Time block your to-do's in your calendar.

1.

2.

3.

What Am I Learning Today?   ## How Am I Serving Others Today?

How Am I Showing Up for Myself Today?

VISUALIZATION
Picture connecting with other women entrepreneurs who understand your journey. Feel a sense of community and shared strength. *Let their support remind you that you're never alone on this path.*

AFFIRMATION
Write at least one positive affirmation that resonates with you today and say it out loud.

DAILY DOSE OF AWESOME
I surround myself with people who support my growth.
Say this affirmation aloud at least seven times and use different inflection points each time.

JOURNAL

Feeling stuck about what to write about today and need some inspiration?
Scan this QR code:

3 Things/People I'm Grateful for Today and why you're grateful for them
ACTION STEP: If you've listed people here, send them a note to tell them.

1.

2.

3.

"To Do's" I'm Committing to Accomplish Today
ACTION STEP: Time block your to-do's in your calendar.

1.

2.

3.

What Am I Learning Today? | How Am I Serving Others Today?

How Am I Showing Up for Myself Today?

VISUALIZATION
Imagine closing out the day with gratitude for all you've balanced. Reflect on each task you've accomplished and feel the pride in juggling it all. *Allow this gratitude to become a source of strength.*

AFFIRMATION
Write at least one positive affirmation that resonates with you today and say it out loud.

DAILY DOSE OF AWESOME
I end my days feeling accomplished and grateful.
Say this affirmation aloud at least seven times and use different inflection points each time.

JOURNAL

DAY 19   /   /

3 Things/People I'm Grateful for Today and why you're grateful for them
ACTION STEP: If you've listed people here, send them a note to tell them.

1.

2.

3.

"To Do's" I'm Committing to Accomplish Today
ACTION STEP: Time block your to-do's in your calendar.

1.

2.

3.

What Am I Learning Today?

How Am I Serving Others Today?

How Am I Showing Up for Myself Today?

VISUALIZATION
See yourself sharing your business vision with a loved one, feeling understood and supported. Imagine their encouragement lifting you up. *Let this reminder of their belief in you strengthen your resolve.*

AFFIRMATION
Write at least one positive affirmation that resonates with you today and say it out loud.

DAILY DOSE OF AWESOME
I celebrate my progress today and know that each step brings me closer to my vision.
Say this affirmation aloud at least seven times and use different inflection points each time.

JOURNAL

Feeling stuck about what to write about today and need some inspiration?
Scan this QR code:

3 Things/People I'm Grateful for Today and why you're grateful for them
ACTION STEP: If you've listed people here, send them a note to tell them.

1.

2.

3.

"To Do's" I'm Committing to Accomplish Today
ACTION STEP: Time block your to-do's in your calendar.

1.

2.

3.

What Am I Learning Today?	How Am I Serving Others Today?

How Am I Showing Up for Myself Today?

VISUALIZATION
Visualize a potential client discovering your work and feeling aligned with your mission. Picture the connection sparking mutual excitement. *Embrace the feeling that your work is valued and impactful.*

AFFIRMATION
Write at least one positive affirmation that resonates with you today and say it out loud.

DAILY DOSE OF AWESOME
My work attracts those who value and appreciate my mission.
Say this affirmation aloud at least seven times and use different inflection points each time.

JOURNAL

3 Things/People I'm Grateful for Today and why you're grateful for them
ACTION STEP: If you've listed people here, send them a note to tell them.

1.

2.

3.

"To Do's" I'm Committing to Accomplish Today
ACTION STEP: Time block your to-do's in your calendar.

1.

2.

3.

What Am I Learning Today?

How Am I Serving Others Today?

How Am I Showing Up for Myself Today?

VISUALIZATION
Imagine celebrating a small win today, acknowledging each step forward. Feel the joy of recognizing your growth, no matter how small. *Allow yourself to celebrate all progress as you work toward your vision.*

AFFIRMATION
Write at least one positive affirmation that resonates with you today and say it out loud.

DAILY DOSE OF AWESOME
I celebrate myself and each step forward, big or small.
Say this affirmation aloud at least seven times and use different inflection points each time.

JOURNAL

Feeling stuck about what to write about today and need some inspiration?
Scan this QR code:

WEEKLY PROGRESS CELEBRATION:
WEED PATROL & PROGRESS TRACKING

Congratulations on another week of growing your Dream Seeds! This **Weekly Progress Celebration** is your time to reflect on all you've accomplished, identify any challenges, and keep your progress on track. Set aside 30 minutes to do a little "weed patrol" and celebrate your wins.

1. Weed Patrol

Take a moment to check in with yourself. **Are there any "weeds" (negative thoughts, self-doubt, or roadblocks) that have sprouted up this week?** Write down anything that has held you back or weighed on you.

Examples of weeds could be:
   + Doubts about your capabilities
   + Negative self-talk
   + Unanticipated obstacles

How will you "nip them in the bud" and keep moving forward? Describe a proactive step or mindset shift to tackle these weeds.

2. Action Review

Reflect on the actions you took during this past week. **Did these actions effectively nurture your Dream Seeds and target outcomes?**

   + What daily actions worked well in nurturing your goals?
   + Were there any actions that felt unproductive or off-track?

List a few adjustments you could make for next week to keep your actions aligned with your vision.

3. Initiative Check

Review the initiatives in your Watering Cans. **Are you on track to achieve each one?** Take a quick look at your key focus areas and consider any adjustments needed.

Which initiatives are moving along well?

Are there any that need a bit more attention or a different approach?

Note any tweaks or new strategies to strengthen your progress next week.

4. Celebrate Success!

Time to celebrate! **What successes or progress can you acknowledge this week?** Whether big or small, every step forward counts. Take a moment to recognize what you've accomplished, and feel proud of yourself for showing up.

+ What are you most proud of this week?

+ How can you reward yourself or simply honor your efforts?

Remember, progress isn't always about huge leaps—it's about steady, consistent steps forward. Give yourself credit for every victory.

3 Things/People I'm Grateful for Today and why you're grateful for them
ACTION STEP: If you've listed people here, send them a note to tell them.

1.

2.

3.

"To Do's" I'm Committing to Accomplish Today
ACTION STEP: Time block your to-do's in your calendar.

1.

2.

3.

What Am I Learning Today? | How Am I Serving Others Today?

How Am I Showing Up for Myself Today?

VISUALIZATION

See your family and friends cheering you on in your business journey. Picture their faces filled with pride. *Let this love and support fuel you to pursue your dreams with confidence.*

AFFIRMATION

Write at least one positive affirmation that resonates with you today and say it out loud.

DAILY DOSE OF AWESOME

I am surrounded by love, support, and encouragement.

Say this affirmation aloud at least seven times and use different inflection points each time.

JOURNAL

3 Things/People I'm Grateful for Today and why you're grateful for them
ACTION STEP: If you've listed people here, send them a note to tell them.

1.

2.

3.

"To Do's" I'm Committing to Accomplish Today
ACTION STEP: Time block your to-do's in your calendar.

1.

2.

3.

What Am I Learning Today?	How Am I Serving Others Today?

How Am I Showing Up for Myself Today?

VISUALIZATION

Visualize yourself confidently asking for help when you need it. Feel the empowerment of leaning on others. *Embrace the strength that comes from collaboration.*

AFFIRMATION

Write at least one positive affirmation that resonates with you today and say it out loud.

DAILY DOSE OF AWESOME

I ask for help with confidence, knowing I deserve support.

Say this affirmation aloud at least seven times and use different inflection points each time.

JOURNAL

3 Things/People I'm Grateful for Today and why you're grateful for them
ACTION STEP: If you've listed people here, send them a note to tell them.

1.

2.

3.

"To Do's" I'm Committing to Accomplish Today
ACTION STEP: Time block your to-do's in your calendar.

1.

2.

3.

What Am I Learning Today?

How Am I Serving Others Today?

How Am I Showing Up for Myself Today?

VISUALIZATION

Imagine wrapping up your day with every item on your to-do list complete. Feel the sense of freedom. *Let this accomplishment remind you of your ability to create the life you desire.*

AFFIRMATION
Write at least one positive affirmation that resonates with you today and say it out loud.

DAILY DOSE OF AWESOME
I am capable of achieving all that I commit to.
Say this affirmation aloud at least seven times and use different inflection points each time.

JOURNAL

Feeling stuck about what to write about today and need some inspiration?
Scan this QR code:

DAY 25   /   /

3 Things/People I'm Grateful for Today and why you're grateful for them
ACTION STEP: If you've listed people here, send them a note to tell them.

1.

2.

3.

"To Do's" I'm Committing to Accomplish Today
ACTION STEP: Time block your to-do's in your calendar.

1.

2.

3.

What Am I Learning Today?

How Am I Serving Others Today?

How Am I Showing Up for Myself Today?

VISUALIZATION
Picture yourself mentally and physically re-charged as you take time for self-care. Feel the energy and clarity that comes from prior-itizing yourself. *Remember to allow self-care to become a non-negotiable part of your journey.*

AFFIRMATION
Write at least one positive affirmation that resonates with you today and say it out loud.

DAILY DOSE OF AWESOME
I am worthy of all good things life has to offer.
Say this affirmation aloud at least seven times and use different inflection points each time.

JOURNAL

3 Things/People I'm Grateful for Today and why you're grateful for them
ACTION STEP: If you've listed people here, send them a note to tell them.

1.

2.

3.

"To Do's" I'm Committing to Accomplish Today
ACTION STEP: Time block your to-do's in your calendar.

1.

2.

3.

What Am I Learning Today?   ## How Am I Serving Others Today?

How Am I Showing Up for Myself Today?

VISUALIZATION

Visualize giving yourself credit for all you've accomplished so far. Let the feeling of pride settle within you. *Acknowledge that your efforts have brought you here and will carry you forward.*

AFFIRMATION

Write at least one positive affirmation that resonates with you today and say it out loud.

DAILY DOSE OF AWESOME

I honor myself and am proud of my accomplishments.

Say this affirmation aloud at least seven times and use different inflection points each time.

JOURNAL

Feeling stuck about what to write about today and need some inspiration?
Scan this QR code:

3 Things/People I'm Grateful for Today and why you're grateful for them
ACTION STEP: If you've listed people here, send them a note to tell them.

1.

2.

3.

"To Do's" I'm Committing to Accomplish Today
ACTION STEP: Time block your to-do's in your calendar.

1.

2.

3.

What Am I Learning Today?	How Am I Serving Others Today?

How Am I Showing Up for Myself Today?

VISUALIZATION
Imagine your work making a meaningful difference in someone's life. Picture the positive impact you're creating. *Allow this vision to remind you of the purpose behind your business.*

AFFIRMATION
Write at least one positive affirmation that resonates with you today and say it out loud.

DAILY DOSE OF AWESOME
My work positively impacts those I serve.
Say this affirmation aloud at least seven times and use different inflection points each time.

JOURNAL

Feeling stuck about what to write about today and need some inspiration?
Scan this QR code:

3 Things/People I'm Grateful for Today and why you're grateful for them
ACTION STEP: If you've listed people here, send them a note to tell them.

1.
2.
3.

"To Do's" I'm Committing to Accomplish Today
ACTION STEP: Time block your to-do's in your calendar.

1.
2.
3.

What Am I Learning Today?

How Am I Serving Others Today?

How Am I Showing Up for Myself Today?

VISUALIZATION
See yourself ending your day with a quiet moment of gratitude. Reflect on all you've done and feel thankful. *Let this sense of appreciation remind you of the value of your journey.*

AFFIRMATION
Write at least one positive affirmation that resonates with you today and say it out loud.

DAILY DOSE OF AWESOME
I am grateful for everything in my life.
Say this affirmation aloud at least seven times and use different inflection points each time.

JOURNAL

WEEKLY PROGRESS CELEBRATION:
WEED PATROL & PROGRESS TRACKING

Congratulations on another week of growing your Dream Seeds! This **Weekly Progress Celebration** is your time to reflect on all you've accomplished, identify any challenges, and keep your progress on track. Set aside 30 minutes to do a little "weed patrol" and celebrate your wins.

1. Weed Patrol

Take a moment to check in with yourself. **Are there any "weeds" (negative thoughts, self-doubt, or roadblocks) that have sprouted up this week?** Write down anything that has held you back or weighed on you.

Examples of weeds could be:
+ Doubts about your capabilities
+ Negative self-talk
+ Unanticipated obstacles

How will you "nip them in the bud" and keep moving forward? Describe a pro-active step or mindset shift to tackle these weeds.

2. Action Review

Reflect on the actions you took during this past week. **Did these actions effectively nurture your Dream Seeds and target outcomes?**
+ What daily actions worked well in nurturing your goals?
+ Were there any actions that felt unproductive or off-track?

List a few adjustments you could make for next week to keep your actions aligned with your vision.

3. Initiative Check

Review the initiatives in your Watering Cans. **Are you on track to achieve each one?** Take a quick look at your key focus areas and consider any adjustments needed.

Which initiatives are moving along well?

Are there any that need a bit more attention or a different approach?

Note any tweaks or new strategies to strengthen your progress next week.

---

4. Celebrate Success!

Time to celebrate! **What successes or progress can you acknowledge this week?** Whether big or small, every step forward counts. Take a moment to recognize what you've accomplished, and feel proud of yourself for showing up.

- + What are you most proud of this week?
- + How can you reward yourself or simply honor your efforts?

Remember, progress isn't always about huge leaps—it's about steady, consistent steps forward. Give yourself credit for every victory.

---

3 Things/People I'm Grateful for Today and why you're grateful for them
ACTION STEP: If you've listed people here, send them a note to tell them.

1.

2.

3.

"To Do's" I'm Committing to Accomplish Today
ACTION STEP: Time block your to-do's in your calendar.

1.

2.

3.

What Am I Learning Today?

How Am I Serving Others Today?

How Am I Showing Up for Myself Today?

VISUALIZATION
Visualize your personal and professional life thriving side by side. See the harmony you're creating through dedication and balance. *Embrace the feeling that you can nurture both with intention.*

AFFIRMATION
Write at least one positive affirmation that resonates with you today and say it out loud.

DAILY DOSE OF AWESOME
I am creating harmony between my family and my business.
Say this affirmation aloud at least seven times and use different inflection points each time.

JOURNAL

Feeling stuck about what to write about today and need some inspiration?
Scan this QR code:

3 Things/People I'm Grateful for Today and why you're grateful for them
ACTION STEP: If you've listed people here, send them a note to tell them.

1.

2.

3.

"To Do's" I'm Committing to Accomplish Today
ACTION STEP: Time block your to-do's in your calendar.

1.

2.

3.

What Am I Learning Today?   How Am I Serving Others Today?

How Am I Showing Up for Myself Today?

VISUALIZATION

Picture yourself prioritizing time with your loved ones without distraction. Feel the peace of being fully present. *Let this reminder of connection reinforce your commitment to balance.*

AFFIRMATION

Write at least one positive affirmation that resonates with you today and say it out loud.

DAILY DOSE OF AWESOME

I am free from distractions and fully present in every moment of my day.

Say this affirmation aloud at least seven times and use different inflection points each time.

JOURNAL

DAY 30 | MONTHLY PRUNING

Set aside 60 minutes to reflect and refocus. Grab your metaphorical pruning shears and assess the bigger picture.

1. Growth Assessment

+ Which Dream Seeds (target outcomes) have shown strong progress? Describe what's working well.
+ Are there any initiatives that haven't yielded the results you expected? What factors might be holding them back?

2. Refinement

+ Have your circumstances or priorities shifted in the last 30 days? If so, how might this impact your key focus areas?
+ Based on what you've learned, is there a specific Dream Seed or focus area that could benefit from refinement?

3. Course Correction

+ Reflect on any unexpected challenges you encountered. What "weeds" (problems) have cropped up that need attention?
+ What actions can you take to address these issues or prevent similar ones from arising?

4. Nourishment Planning

+ Check in on your mindset. Could you strengthen areas of your mental well-being by increasing confidence or managing stress more effectively?
+ Schedule at least one activity this week to nurture and nourish your mind. Describe what you'll do and why.

3 Things/People I'm Grateful for Today and why you're grateful for them
ACTION STEP: If you've listed people here, send them a note to tell them.

1.

2.

3.

"To Do's" I'm Committing to Accomplish Today
ACTION STEP: Time block your to-do's in your calendar.

1.

2.

3.

What Am I Learning Today?	How Am I Serving Others Today?

How Am I Showing Up for Myself Today?

VISUALIZATION
Imagine yourself confidently networking with like-minded people. See new doors of opportunity opening. *Embrace the excitement of connecting with those who inspire you.*

AFFIRMATION
Write at least one positive affirmation that resonates with you today and say it out loud.

DAILY DOSE OF AWESOME
I actively build a supportive network that uplifts and inspires my growth.
Say this affirmation aloud at least seven times and use different inflection points each time.

JOURNAL

Feeling stuck about what to write about today and need some inspiration?
Scan this QR code:

3 Things/People I'm Grateful for Today and why you're grateful for them
ACTION STEP: If you've listed people here, send them a note to tell them.

1.

2.

3.

"To Do's" I'm Committing to Accomplish Today
ACTION STEP: Time block your to-do's in your calendar.

1.

2.

3.

What Am I Learning Today?   ## How Am I Serving Others Today?

How Am I Showing Up for Myself Today?

VISUALIZATION
Visualize yourself handling a busy day with focus and resilience. See each task flowing smoothly. *Let this calm determination guide you through your responsibilities.*

AFFIRMATION
Write at least one positive affirmation that resonates with you today and say it out loud.

DAILY DOSE OF AWESOME
I handle my responsibilities
with ease and grace.
Say this affirmation aloud at least seven times and
use different inflection points each time.

JOURNAL

Feeling stuck about what to write about today and need some inspiration?
Scan this QR code:

3 Things/People I'm Grateful for Today and why you're grateful for them
ACTION STEP: If you've listed people here, send them a note to tell them.

1.

2.

3.

"To Do's" I'm Committing to Accomplish Today
ACTION STEP: Time block your to-do's in your calendar.

1.

2.

3.

What Am I Learning Today? | ## How Am I Serving Others Today?

How Am I Showing Up for Myself Today?

VISUALIZATION
Picture yourself in a moment of self-reflection, honoring your journey so far. Feel proud of your growth and resilience. *Let this acknowledgment fuel you for the next step.*

AFFIRMATION
Write at least one positive affirmation that resonates with you today and say it out loud.

DAILY DOSE OF AWESOME
I honor my journey and all
the growth it brings.
Say this affirmation aloud at least seven times and use different inflection points each time.

JOURNAL

Feeling stuck about what to write about today and need some inspiration?
Scan this QR code:

3 Things/People I'm Grateful for Today and why you're grateful for them
ACTION STEP: If you've listed people here, send them a note to tell them.

1.

2.

3.

"To Do's" I'm Committing to Accomplish Today
ACTION STEP: Time block your to-do's in your calendar.

1.

2.

3.

What Am I Learning Today?

How Am I Serving Others Today?

How Am I Showing Up for Myself Today?

VISUALIZATION

Imagine being fully present with your friends and family, knowing you're creating lasting memories. Feel the love and joy of this shared moment. *Hold onto this as a reminder of what matters most.*

AFFIRMATION

Write at least one positive affirmation that resonates with you today and say it out loud.

DAILY DOSE OF AWESOME

I prioritize creating lasting memories with my loved ones.

Say this affirmation aloud at least seven times and use different inflection points each time.

JOURNAL

3 Things/People I'm Grateful for Today and why you're grateful for them
ACTION STEP: If you've listed people here, send them a note to tell them.

1.
2.
3.

"To Do's" I'm Committing to Accomplish Today
ACTION STEP: Time block your to-do's in your calendar.

1.
2.
3.

What Am I Learning Today?	How Am I Serving Others Today?

How Am I Showing Up for Myself Today?

VISUALIZATION
Visualize overcoming a fear or doubt holding you back. See yourself taking that step confidently. *Embrace the freedom that comes from letting go of what no longer serves you.*

AFFIRMATION
Write at least one positive affirmation that resonates with you today and say it out loud.

DAILY DOSE OF AWESOME
I release any fears holding me back and step forward with courage.
Say this affirmation aloud at least seven times and use different inflection points each time.

JOURNAL

Feeling stuck about what to write about today and need some inspiration?
Scan this QR code:

WEEKLY PROGRESS CELEBRATION:
WEED PATROL & PROGRESS TRACKING

Congratulations on another week of growing your Dream Seeds! This **Weekly Progress Celebration** is your time to reflect on all you've accomplished, identify any challenges, and keep your progress on track. Set aside 30 minutes to do a little "weed patrol" and celebrate your wins.

1. Weed Patrol

Take a moment to check in with yourself. **Are there any "weeds" (negative thoughts, self-doubt, or roadblocks) that have sprouted up this week?** Write down anything that has held you back or weighed on you.

Examples of weeds could be:
+ Doubts about your capabilities
+ Negative self-talk
+ Unanticipated obstacles

How will you "nip them in the bud" and keep moving forward? Describe a proactive step or mindset shift to tackle these weeds.

2. Action Review

Reflect on the actions you took during this past week. **Did these actions effectively nurture your Dream Seeds and target outcomes?**

+ What daily actions worked well in nurturing your goals?
+ Were there any actions that felt unproductive or off-track?

List a few adjustments you could make for next week to keep your actions aligned with your vision.

3. Initiative Check

Review the initiatives in your Watering Cans. **Are you on track to achieve each one?** Take a quick look at your key focus areas and consider any adjustments needed.

Which initiatives are moving along well?

Are there any that need a bit more attention or a different approach?

Note any tweaks or new strategies to strengthen your progress next week.

_____

_____

_____

_____

4. Celebrate Success!

Time to celebrate! **What successes or progress can you acknowledge this week?** Whether big or small, every step forward counts. Take a moment to recognize what you've accomplished, and feel proud of yourself for showing up.

+ What are you most proud of this week?
+ How can you reward yourself or simply honor your efforts?

Remember, progress isn't always about huge leaps—it's about steady, consistent steps forward. Give yourself credit for every victory.

_____

_____

_____

_____

3 Things/People I'm Grateful for Today and why you're grateful for them
ACTION STEP: If you've listed people here, send them a note to tell them.

1.

2.

3.

"To Do's" I'm Committing to Accomplish Today
ACTION STEP: Time block your to-do's in your calendar.

1.

2.

3.

What Am I Learning Today?

How Am I Serving Others Today?

How Am I Showing Up for Myself Today?

VISUALIZATION
Picture yourself listening attentively to a loved one, offering support and empathy. Feel the closeness in this connection. *Let this act of kindness remind you of the impact you have in their lives.*

AFFIRMATION
Write at least one positive affirmation that resonates with you today and say it out loud.

DAILY DOSE OF AWESOME
I create strong, meaningful connections with those around me.
Say this affirmation aloud at least seven times and use different inflection points each time.

JOURNAL

3 Things/People I'm Grateful for Today and why you're grateful for them
ACTION STEP: If you've listed people here, send them a note to tell them.

1.

2.

3.

"To Do's" I'm Committing to Accomplish Today
ACTION STEP: Time block your to-do's in your calendar.

1.

2.

3.

What Am I Learning Today?	How Am I Serving Others Today?

How Am I Showing Up for Myself Today?

VISUALIZATION
See yourself starting the day with a clear plan and a positive mindset. Feel the sense of control and confidence it brings. *Let this clarity guide you through each hour.*

AFFIRMATION
Write at least one positive affirmation that resonates with you today and say it out loud.

DAILY DOSE OF AWESOME
I start today with clarity, focus, and purpose.

Say this affirmation aloud at least seven times and use different inflection points each time.

JOURNAL

3 Things/People I'm Grateful for Today and why you're grateful for them
ACTION STEP: If you've listed people here, send them a note to tell them.

1.

2.

3.

"To Do's" I'm Committing to Accomplish Today
ACTION STEP: Time block your to-do's in your calendar.

1.

2.

3.

What Am I Learning Today?	How Am I Serving Others Today?

How Am I Showing Up for Myself Today?

VISUALIZATION
Visualize hitting a milestone in your business. Feel the joy and pride of your accomplishment. *Allow this success to energize your commitment to your vision.*

AFFIRMATION
Write at least one positive affirmation that resonates with you today and say it out loud.

DAILY DOSE OF AWESOME
I am proud of myself.
Say this affirmation aloud at least seven times and use different inflection points each time.

JOURNAL

3 Things/People I'm Grateful for Today and why you're grateful for them
ACTION STEP: If you've listed people here, send them a note to tell them.

1.
2.
3.

"To Do's" I'm Committing to Accomplish Today
ACTION STEP: Time block your to-do's in your calendar.

1.
2.
3.

What Am I Learning Today?	How Am I Serving Others Today?

How Am I Showing Up for Myself Today?

VISUALIZATION
Imagine a day free from distractions, where you focus fully on what matters. See how much you accomplish and how good it feels. *Let this sense of fulfillment motivate you to create boundaries.*

AFFIRMATION
Write at least one positive affirmation that resonates with you today and say it out loud.

DAILY DOSE OF AWESOME
I protect my time and focus on what truly matters.
Say this affirmation aloud at least seven times and use different inflection points each time.

JOURNAL

DAY 40   /   /

3 Things/People I'm Grateful for Today and why you're grateful for them
ACTION STEP: If you've listed people here, send them a note to tell them.

1.

2.

3.

"To Do's" I'm Committing to Accomplish Today
ACTION STEP: Time block your to-do's in your calendar.

1.

2.

3.

What Am I Learning Today?	How Am I Serving Others Today?

How Am I Showing Up for Myself Today?

VISUALIZATION
Picture yourself in a moment of deep relaxation, knowing you've earned it. Feel the tension melt away. *Allow this peace to renew your strength and resolve.*

AFFIRMATION
Write at least one positive affirmation that resonates with you today and say it out loud.

DAILY DOSE OF AWESOME
I embrace moments of rest
and feel fully recharged.
Say this affirmation aloud at least seven times and use different inflection points each time.

JOURNAL

3 Things/People I'm Grateful for Today and why you're grateful for them
ACTION STEP: If you've listed people here, send them a note to tell them.

1.

2.

3.

"To Do's" I'm Committing to Accomplish Today
ACTION STEP: Time block your to-do's in your calendar.

1.

2.

3.

What Am I Learning Today?	How Am I Serving Others Today?

How Am I Showing Up for Myself Today?

VISUALIZATION
See yourself delegating tasks that drain your energy. Imagine the freedom and space it creates for what matters most to you. *Embrace the power of letting go to make room for growth.*

AFFIRMATION
Write at least one positive affirmation that resonates with you today and say it out loud.

DAILY DOSE OF AWESOME
I delegate confidently, creating space for what I love.
Say this affirmation aloud at least seven times and use different inflection points each time.

JOURNAL

Feeling stuck about what to write about today and need some inspiration?
Scan this QR code:

3 Things/People I'm Grateful for Today and why you're grateful for them
ACTION STEP: If you've listed people here, send them a note to tell them.

1.

2.

3.

"To Do's" I'm Committing to Accomplish Today
ACTION STEP: Time block your to-do's in your calendar.

1.

2.

3.

What Am I Learning Today?

How Am I Serving Others Today?

How Am I Showing Up for Myself Today?

VISUALIZATION

Visualize setting boundaries that protect your personal time. Feel the empowerment of prioritizing yourself and your well-being. *Let this commitment to balance guide your actions.*

AFFIRMATION

Write at least one positive affirmation that resonates with you today and say it out loud.

DAILY DOSE OF AWESOME

I set healthy boundaries that honor my well-being.

Say this affirmation aloud at least seven times and use different inflection points each time.

JOURNAL

WEEKLY PROGRESS CELEBRATION:
WEED PATROL & PROGRESS TRACKING

Congratulations on another week of growing your Dream Seeds! This **Weekly Progress Celebration** is your time to reflect on all you've accomplished, identify any challenges, and keep your progress on track. Set aside 30 minutes to do a little "weed patrol" and celebrate your wins.

1. Weed Patrol

Take a moment to check in with yourself. **Are there any "weeds" (negative thoughts, self-doubt, or roadblocks) that have sprouted up this week?** Write down anything that has held you back or weighed on you.

Examples of weeds could be:
- Doubts about your capabilities
- Negative self-talk
- Unanticipated obstacles

How will you "nip them in the bud" and keep moving forward? Describe a proactive step or mindset shift to tackle these weeds.

2. Action Review

Reflect on the actions you took during this past week. **Did these actions effectively nurture your Dream Seeds and target outcomes?**

- What daily actions worked well in nurturing your goals?
- Were there any actions that felt unproductive or off-track?

List a few adjustments you could make for next week to keep your actions aligned with your vision.

3. Initiative Check

Review the initiatives in your Watering Cans. **Are you on track to achieve each one?** Take a quick look at your key focus areas and consider any adjustments needed.

Which initiatives are moving along well?

Are there any that need a bit more attention or a different approach?

Note any tweaks or new strategies to strengthen your progress next week.

4. Celebrate Success!

Time to celebrate! **What successes or progress can you acknowledge this week?** Whether big or small, every step forward counts. Take a moment to recognize what you've accomplished, and feel proud of yourself for showing up.

+ What are you most proud of this week?

+ How can you reward yourself or simply honor your efforts?

Remember, progress isn't always about huge leaps—it's about steady, consistent steps forward. Give yourself credit for every victory.

3 Things/People I'm Grateful for Today and why you're grateful for them
ACTION STEP: If you've listed people here, send them a note to tell them.

1.

2.

3.

"To Do's" I'm Committing to Accomplish Today
ACTION STEP: Time block your to-do's in your calendar.

1.

2.

3.

What Am I Learning Today? | ## How Am I Serving Others Today?

How Am I Showing Up for Myself Today?

VISUALIZATION
Imagine receiving heartfelt feedback from a client who values your work. Feel the validation and pride. *Let this reminder of your impact motivate you to keep pushing forward.*

AFFIRMATION
Write at least one positive affirmation that resonates with you today and say it out loud.

DAILY DOSE OF AWESOME
I deliver work that is valuable and meaningful, attracting clients and partners who appreciate my contributions.
Say this affirmation aloud at least seven times and use different inflection points each time.

JOURNAL

Feeling stuck about what to write about today and need some inspiration?
Scan this QR code:

3 Things/People I'm Grateful for Today and why you're grateful for them
ACTION STEP: If you've listed people here, send them a note to tell them.

1.

2.

3.

"To Do's" I'm Committing to Accomplish Today
ACTION STEP: Time block your to-do's in your calendar.

1.

2.

3.

What Am I Learning Today?

How Am I Serving Others Today?

How Am I Showing Up for Myself Today?

VISUALIZATION
Picture yourself in a moment of pure joy with your loved ones. Feel the warmth of their love and support. *Let this connection ground you and bring perspective to your work.*

AFFIRMATION
Write at least one positive affirmation that resonates with you today and say it out loud.

DAILY DOSE OF AWESOME
I cherish joyful moments with my family and friends.
Say this affirmation aloud at least seven times and use different inflection points each time.

JOURNAL

Feeling stuck about what to write about today and need some inspiration?
Scan this QR code:

3 Things/People I'm Grateful for Today and why you're grateful for them
ACTION STEP: If you've listed people here, send them a note to tell them.

1.

2.

3.

"To Do's" I'm Committing to Accomplish Today
ACTION STEP: Time block your to-do's in your calendar.

1.

2.

3.

What Am I Learning Today?   How Am I Serving Others Today?

How Am I Showing Up for Myself Today?

VISUALIZATION
Visualize yourself taking on a new challenge with courage. Feel the thrill of stepping out of your comfort zone. *Let this experience remind you of your boundless potential.*

AFFIRMATION
Write at least one positive affirmation that resonates with you today and say it out loud.

DAILY DOSE OF AWESOME
I embrace new challenges with excitement and courage.
Say this affirmation aloud at least seven times and use different inflection points each time.

JOURNAL

3 Things/People I'm Grateful for Today and why you're grateful for them
ACTION STEP: If you've listed people here, send them a note to tell them.

1. ....

2. ....

3. ....

"To Do's" I'm Committing to Accomplish Today
ACTION STEP: Time block your to-do's in your calendar.

1. ....

2. ....

3. ....

What Am I Learning Today?	How Am I Serving Others Today?

How Am I Showing Up for Myself Today?

....

....

VISUALIZATION
Imagine giving yourself permission to rest and recharge. Feel the energy and calm it brings. *Embrace self-care as a necessary part of your success.*

AFFIRMATION
Write at least one positive affirmation that resonates with you today and say it out loud.

....

....

....

....

....

DAILY DOSE OF AWESOME
I deserve rest, and I give myself permission to recharge.
Say this affirmation aloud at least seven times and use different inflection points each time.

JOURNAL

DAY 47   /   /

3 Things/People I'm Grateful for Today and why you're grateful for them
ACTION STEP: If you've listed people here, send them a note to tell them.

1.

2.

3.

"To Do's" I'm Committing to Accomplish Today
ACTION STEP: Time block your to-do's in your calendar.

1.

2.

3.

What Am I Learning Today? | How Am I Serving Others Today?

How Am I Showing Up for Myself Today?

VISUALIZATION
See yourself in a day where you accomplish each goal with focus and ease. Feel the satisfaction of seeing everything come together. *Let this accomplishment fuel your motivation.*

AFFIRMATION
Write at least one positive affirmation that resonates with you today and say it out loud.

DAILY DOSE OF AWESOME
I am productive, focused, and in control of my day.
Say this affirmation aloud at least seven times and use different inflection points each time.

JOURNAL

3 Things/People I'm Grateful for Today and why you're grateful for them
ACTION STEP: If you've listed people here, send them a note to tell them.

1.

2.

3.

"To Do's" I'm Committing to Accomplish Today
ACTION STEP: Time block your to-do's in your calendar.

1.

2.

3.

What Am I Learning Today?

How Am I Serving Others Today?

How Am I Showing Up for Myself Today?

VISUALIZATION
Visualize a client or team member expressing gratitude for your support. Feel the impact you're making through your work. *Allow this appreciation to remind you of your purpose.*

AFFIRMATION
Write at least one positive affirmation that resonates with you today and say it out loud.

DAILY DOSE OF AWESOME
The impact of my work brings me fulfillment and pride.
Say this affirmation aloud at least seven times and use different inflection points each time.

JOURNAL

Feeling stuck about what to write about today and need some inspiration?
Scan this QR code:

3 Things/People I'm Grateful for Today and why you're grateful for them
ACTION STEP: If you've listed people here, send them a note to tell them.

1.

2.

3.

"To Do's" I'm Committing to Accomplish Today
ACTION STEP: Time block your to-do's in your calendar.

1.

2.

3.

What Am I Learning Today?

How Am I Serving Others Today?

How Am I Showing Up for Myself Today?

VISUALIZATION
Imagine reaching the end of a successful day, grateful for each moment. Feel the peace of accomplishment and balance. *Let this feeling inspire you to live each day intentionally.*

AFFIRMATION
Write at least one positive affirmation that resonates with you today and say it out loud.

DAILY DOSE OF AWESOME
I am grateful for each achievement and each step forward.
Say this affirmation aloud at least seven times and use different inflection points each time.

JOURNAL

Feeling stuck about what to write about today and need some inspiration?
Scan this QR code:

WEEKLY PROGRESS CELEBRATION:
WEED PATROL & PROGRESS TRACKING

Congratulations on another week of growing your Dream Seeds! This **Weekly Progress Celebration** is your time to reflect on all you've accomplished, identify any challenges, and keep your progress on track. Set aside 30 minutes to do a little "weed patrol" and celebrate your wins.

1. Weed Patrol

Take a moment to check in with yourself. **Are there any "weeds" (negative thoughts, self-doubt, or roadblocks) that have sprouted up this week?** Write down anything that has held you back or weighed on you.

Examples of weeds could be:
+ Doubts about your capabilities
+ Negative self-talk
+ Unanticipated obstacles

How will you "nip them in the bud" and keep moving forward? Describe a proactive step or mindset shift to tackle these weeds.

2. Action Review

Reflect on the actions you took during this past week. **Did these actions effectively nurture your Dream Seeds and target outcomes?**

+ What daily actions worked well in nurturing your goals?
+ Were there any actions that felt unproductive or off-track?

List a few adjustments you could make for next week to keep your actions aligned with your vision.

3. Initiative Check

Review the initiatives in your Watering Cans. **Are you on track to achieve each one?** Take a quick look at your key focus areas and consider any adjustments needed.

Which initiatives are moving along well?

Are there any that need a bit more attention or a different approach?

Note any tweaks or new strategies to strengthen your progress next week.

---

4. Celebrate Success!

Time to celebrate! **What successes or progress can you acknowledge this week?** Whether big or small, every step forward counts. Take a moment to recognize what you've accomplished, and feel proud of yourself for showing up.

- ◆ What are you most proud of this week?
- ◆ How can you reward yourself or simply honor your efforts?

Remember, progress isn't always about huge leaps—it's about steady, consistent steps forward. Give yourself credit for every victory.

DAY 50   /   /

3 Things/People I'm Grateful for Today and why you're grateful for them
ACTION STEP: If you've listed people here, send them a note to tell them.

1.

2.

3.

"To Do's" I'm Committing to Accomplish Today
ACTION STEP: Time block your to-do's in your calendar.

1.

2.

3.

What Am I Learning Today?

How Am I Serving Others Today?

How Am I Showing Up for Myself Today?

VISUALIZATION
Picture yourself confidently navigating a busy schedule, staying calm and focused. Embrace the balance and control you feel. *Let this sense of poise guide you through each task.*

AFFIRMATION
Write at least one positive affirmation that resonates with you today and say it out loud.

DAILY DOSE OF AWESOME
I move through busy days with calm and focus.
Say this affirmation aloud at least seven times and use different inflection points each time.

JOURNAL

Feeling stuck about what to write about today and need some inspiration?
Scan this QR code:

3 Things/People I'm Grateful for Today and why you're grateful for them
ACTION STEP: If you've listed people here, send them a note to tell them.

1.

2.

3.

"To Do's" I'm Committing to Accomplish Today
ACTION STEP: Time block your to-do's in your calendar.

1.

2.

3.

What Am I Learning Today?

How Am I Serving Others Today?

How Am I Showing Up for Myself Today?

VISUALIZATION
Envision how your business will support the lifestyle you desire. Picture the freedom, stability, and joy it brings. *Feel the alignment between your work and the life you're building.*

AFFIRMATION
Write at least one positive affirmation that resonates with you today and say it out loud.

DAILY DOSE OF AWESOME
My business supports the lifestyle I desire.
Say this affirmation aloud at least seven times and use different inflection points each time.

JOURNAL

3 Things/People I'm Grateful for Today and why you're grateful for them
ACTION STEP: If you've listed people here, send them a note to tell them.

1.

2.

3.

"To Do's" I'm Committing to Accomplish Today
ACTION STEP: Time block your to-do's in your calendar.

1.

2.

3.

What Am I Learning Today?

How Am I Serving Others Today?

How Am I Showing Up for Myself Today?

VISUALIZATION

Visualize your family sharing a meal together, filled with laughter and love. Imagine the warmth and connection in the room. *Embrace this as a reminder of the importance of creating these moments.*

AFFIRMATION

Write at least one positive affirmation that resonates with you today and say it out loud.

DAILY DOSE OF AWESOME

I create moments of joy and connection with my family, building memories that enrich our lives.

Say this affirmation aloud at least seven times and use different inflection points each time.

JOURNAL

Feeling stuck about what to write about today and need some inspiration?
Scan this QR code:

3 Things/People I'm Grateful for Today and why you're grateful for them
ACTION STEP: If you've listed people here, send them a note to tell them.

1.

2.

3.

"To Do's" I'm Committing to Accomplish Today
ACTION STEP: Time block your to-do's in your calendar.

1.

2.

3.

What Am I Learning Today?

How Am I Serving Others Today?

How Am I Showing Up for Myself Today?

VISUALIZATION
Picture yourself meeting a financial target you've set for this quarter. Feel the pride and satisfaction of achieving it. *Let this success boost your confidence in setting and reaching bigger outcomes.*

AFFIRMATION
Write at least one positive affirmation that resonates with you today and say it out loud.

DAILY DOSE OF AWESOME
I am proud of reaching my financial goals.
Say this affirmation aloud at least seven times and use different inflection points each time.

JOURNAL

Feeling stuck about what to write about today and need some inspiration?
Scan this QR code:

3 Things/People I'm Grateful for Today and why you're grateful for them
ACTION STEP: If you've listed people here, send them a note to tell them.

1.

2.

3.

"To Do's" I'm Committing to Accomplish Today
ACTION STEP: Time block your to-do's in your calendar.

1.

2.

3.

What Am I Learning Today? | How Am I Serving Others Today?

How Am I Showing Up for Myself Today?

VISUALIZATION

Imagine that you're exactly where you need to be today. Embrace a sense of contentment and trust in your journey. *Allow this feeling of alignment to bring peace and confidence to your day.*

AFFIRMATION

Write at least one positive affirmation that resonates with you today and say it out loud.

DAILY DOSE OF AWESOME
I trust that I am exactly where I need to be.
Say this affirmation aloud at least seven times and use different inflection points each time.

JOURNAL

Feeling stuck about what to write about today and need some inspiration?
Scan this QR code:

3 Things/People I'm Grateful for Today and why you're grateful for them
ACTION STEP: If you've listed people here, send them a note to tell them.

1.

2.

3.

"To Do's" I'm Committing to Accomplish Today
ACTION STEP: Time block your to-do's in your calendar.

1.

2.

3.

What Am I Learning Today?	How Am I Serving Others Today?

How Am I Showing Up for Myself Today?

VISUALIZATION
Envision starting tomorrow with excitement for what's ahead. Picture yourself waking up energized and ready to make progress. *Let this anticipation inspire you to take intentional steps today.*

AFFIRMATION
Write at least one positive affirmation that resonates with you today and say it out loud.

DAILY DOSE OF AWESOME
I am excited and grateful for the opportunities ahead of me.
Say this affirmation aloud at least seven times and use different inflection points each time.

JOURNAL

Feeling stuck about what to write about today and need some inspiration?
Scan this QR code:

DAY 56   /   /

3 Things/People I'm Grateful for Today and why you're grateful for them
ACTION STEP: If you've listed people here, send them a note to tell them.

1.

2.

3.

"To Do's" I'm Committing to Accomplish Today
ACTION STEP: Time block your to-do's in your calendar.

1.

2.

3.

What Am I Learning Today?

How Am I Serving Others Today?

How Am I Showing Up for Myself Today?

VISUALIZATION

See yourself confidently introducing your business at an event. Feel the pride of sharing your work with others. *Embrace this confidence as you connect with others in meaningful ways.*

AFFIRMATION

Write at least one positive affirmation that resonates with you today and say it out loud.

DAILY DOSE OF AWESOME

I confidently share my vision and expertise, knowing my work brings value and inspiration to others.

Say this affirmation aloud at least seven times and use different inflection points each time.

JOURNAL

WEEKLY PROGRESS CELEBRATION:
WEED PATROL & PROGRESS TRACKING

Congratulations on another week of growing your Dream Seeds! This **Weekly Progress Celebration** is your time to reflect on all you've accomplished, identify any challenges, and keep your progress on track. Set aside 30 minutes to do a little "weed patrol" and celebrate your wins.

1. Weed Patrol

Take a moment to check in with yourself. **Are there any "weeds" (negative thoughts, self-doubt, or roadblocks) that have sprouted up this week?** Write down anything that has held you back or weighed on you.

Examples of weeds could be:
+ Doubts about your capabilities
+ Negative self-talk
+ Unanticipated obstacles

How will you "nip them in the bud" and keep moving forward? Describe a proactive step or mindset shift to tackle these weeds.

2. Action Review

Reflect on the actions you took during this past week. **Did these actions effectively nurture your Dream Seeds and target outcomes?**

+ What daily actions worked well in nurturing your goals?
+ Were there any actions that felt unproductive or off-track?

List a few adjustments you could make for next week to keep your actions aligned with your vision.

3. Initiative Check

Review the initiatives in your Watering Cans. **Are you on track to achieve each one?** Take a quick look at your key focus areas and consider any adjustments needed.

Which initiatives are moving along well?

Are there any that need a bit more attention or a different approach?

Note any tweaks or new strategies to strengthen your progress next week.

_____

_____

_____

_____

4. Celebrate Success!

Time to celebrate! **What successes or progress can you acknowledge this week?** Whether big or small, every step forward counts. Take a moment to recognize what you've accomplished, and feel proud of yourself for showing up.

+ What are you most proud of this week?
+ How can you reward yourself or simply honor your efforts?

Remember, progress isn't always about huge leaps—it's about steady, consistent steps forward. Give yourself credit for every victory.

_____

_____

_____

_____

3 Things/People I'm Grateful for Today and why you're grateful for them
ACTION STEP: If you've listed people here, send them a note to tell them.

1.

2.

3.

"To Do's" I'm Committing to Accomplish Today
ACTION STEP: Time block your to-do's in your calendar.

1.

2.

3.

What Am I Learning Today?   ## How Am I Serving Others Today?

How Am I Showing Up for Myself Today?

VISUALIZATION
Visualize yourself setting healthy boundaries that allow for personal time without
guilt. Feel the relief and balance it brings. *Let
this commitment to self-care guide you as you
plan your day.*

AFFIRMATION
Write at least one positive affirmation that
resonates with you today and say it out loud.

DAILY DOSE OF AWESOME
I honor my boundaries and
make time for myself.
Say this affirmation aloud at least seven times and
use different inflection points each time.

JOURNAL

Feeling stuck about what to write about today and need some inspiration?
Scan this QR code:

DAY 58   /   /

3 Things/People I'm Grateful for Today and why you're grateful for them
ACTION STEP: If you've listed people here, send them a note to tell them.

1.

2.

3.

"To Do's" I'm Committing to Accomplish Today
ACTION STEP: Time block your to-do's in your calendar.

1.

2.

3.

What Am I Learning Today?

How Am I Serving Others Today?

How Am I Showing Up for Myself Today?

VISUALIZATION

Imagine organizing your week with clear priorities and achievable goals. See yourself moving through each day with purpose. Embrace the sense of control and productivity this brings to your life.

AFFIRMATION

Write at least one positive affirmation that resonates with you today and say it out loud.

DAILY DOSE OF AWESOME
I plan my time with clarity and intention.

Say this affirmation aloud at least seven times and use different inflection points each time.

JOURNAL

Feeling stuck about what to write about today and need some inspiration?
Scan this QR code:

3 Things/People I'm Grateful for Today and why you're grateful for them
ACTION STEP: If you've listed people here, send them a note to tell them.

1.

2.

3.

"To Do's" I'm Committing to Accomplish Today
ACTION STEP: Time block your to-do's in your calendar.

1.

2.

3.

What Am I Learning Today?   ## How Am I Serving Others Today?

How Am I Showing Up for Myself Today?

VISUALIZATION
Envision taking a moment to reflect on how far you've come. Feel proud of the growth, challenges overcome, and lessons learned. *Let this reflection remind you of your resilience and capability.*

AFFIRMATION
Write at least one positive affirmation that resonates with you today and say it out loud.

DAILY DOSE OF AWESOME
I am proud of how far I've come.
Say this affirmation aloud at least seven times and use different inflection points each time.

JOURNAL

Feeling stuck about what to write about today and need some inspiration?
Scan this QR code:

3 Things/People I'm Grateful for Today and why you're grateful for them
ACTION STEP: If you've listed people here, send them a note to tell them.

1.

2.

3.

"To Do's" I'm Committing to Accomplish Today
ACTION STEP: Time block your to-do's in your calendar.

1.

2.

3.

What Am I Learning Today?

How Am I Serving Others Today?

How Am I Showing Up for Myself Today?

VISUALIZATION

See yourself filled with gratitude for the family, friends, and clients supporting you. Imagine each person who has encouraged and uplifted you along your journey. *Feel the warmth of their support and let it remind you that you are surrounded by people who believe in you.*

AFFIRMATION

Write at least one positive affirmation that resonates with you today and say it out loud.

DAILY DOSE OF AWESOME

I am grateful for the family, friends, and clients who support me.

Say this affirmation aloud at least seven times and use different inflection points each time.

JOURNAL

Feeling stuck about what to write about today and need some inspiration?
Scan this QR code:

DAY 60 | MONTHLY PRUNING

Time for another reflection and adjustment session! Use these questions to take stock of where you are and ensure you're aligned with your vision.

1. Growth Assessment

+ Reflect on your progress with each Dream Seed. Which seeds are flourishing, and which ones may need more attention?

+ What accomplishments or milestones have you reached that you're particularly proud of?

2. Refinement

+ Have any of your priorities or circumstances shifted over the last month? If so, what adjustments can you make to your key focus areas?

+ Are there specific areas in your Watering Cans (key focus areas) that need refinement to align with your current situation?

3. Course Correction

+ Identify any challenges or obstacles you faced. What lessons have you learned from these experiences?

+ Consider practical solutions to address any ongoing issues. What course corrections will you make to keep your Dream Seeds on track?

4. Nourishment Planning

+ Assess your current mindset. Are there areas where you need additional support, such as building resilience or reducing stress?

+ Choose one specific activity or habit to nurture your mental well-being this month, and commit to incorporating it. Describe your plan.

DAY 60 | KEEP BUILDING YOUR MOMENTUM—DON'T LOSE A DAY!

Congratulations on reaching Day 60! You're well into your *90-Day Momentum Maker*, building habits, achieving milestones, and creating the life and business you envision. By now, you've experienced the power of focused, consistent action—and this momentum is too valuable to lose.

To keep this energy going strong, it's essential to order your next *90-Day Momentum Maker* now, so it's ready when you are! If you wait until Day 90, you risk a lapse in your habits and a break in your progress. Imagine the feeling of seamlessly continuing your journey on Day 91, without missing a beat!

Head to livebigwithstacey.com/momentum to order your next guide. This way, you'll have everything in place to keep the momentum rolling—no gaps, no pauses, just steady growth.

Your journey is too important to stall. Keep showing up, keep taking action, and keep Living BIG. Let's make sure Day 91 and beyond are even more powerful!

Grab your next *90-Day Momentum Maker* today at livebigwithstacey.com/momentum or scan the QR code:

3 Things/People I'm Grateful for Today and why you're grateful for them
ACTION STEP: If you've listed people here, send them a note to tell them.

1. ....

2. ....

3. ....

"To Do's" I'm Committing to Accomplish Today
ACTION STEP: Time block your to-do's in your calendar.

1. ....

2. ....

3. ....

What Am I Learning Today?	How Am I Serving Others Today?

How Am I Showing Up for Myself Today?

VISUALIZATION
Visualize yourself sharing a major business milestone with your loved ones. Feel their pride and support as they celebrate with you. *Embrace this as a reminder of the impact your work has on both your life and theirs.*

AFFIRMATION
Write at least one positive affirmation that resonates with you today and say it out loud.

DAILY DOSE OF AWESOME
I am surrounded by love and support in every step I take.
Say this affirmation aloud at least seven times and use different inflection points each time.

JOURNAL

3 Things/People I'm Grateful for Today and why you're grateful for them
ACTION STEP: If you've listed people here, send them a note to tell them.

1.

2.

3.

"To Do's" I'm Committing to Accomplish Today
ACTION STEP: Time block your to-do's in your calendar.

1.

2.

3.

What Am I Learning Today?

How Am I Serving Others Today?

How Am I Showing Up for Myself Today?

VISUALIZATION

Picture receiving positive feedback from a client or partner. Feel the joy of being valued for your contributions. *Let this recognition re-affirm your unique gifts and purpose.*

AFFIRMATION

Write at least one positive affirmation that resonates with you today and say it out loud.

DAILY DOSE OF AWESOME

I am valued and respected for my contributions.

Say this affirmation aloud at least seven times and use different inflection points each time.

JOURNAL

3 Things/People I'm Grateful for Today and why you're grateful for them
ACTION STEP: If you've listed people here, send them a note to tell them.

1.

2.

3.

"To Do's" I'm Committing to Accomplish Today
ACTION STEP: Time block your to-do's in your calendar.

1.

2.

3.

What Am I Learning Today?   How Am I Serving Others Today?

How Am I Showing Up for Myself Today?

VISUALIZATION
Imagine a family celebration honoring both your achievements and togetherness. Feel the warmth and love that come from shared success. *Hold onto this moment as a reminder of your "why."*

AFFIRMATION
Write at least one positive affirmation that resonates with you today and say it out loud.

DAILY DOSE OF AWESOME
I celebrate my achievements with those I love.
Say this affirmation aloud at least seven times and use different inflection points each time.

JOURNAL

Feeling stuck about what to write about today and need some inspiration?
Scan this QR code:

WEEKLY PROGRESS CELEBRATION:
WEED PATROL & PROGRESS TRACKING

Congratulations on another week of growing your Dream Seeds! This **Weekly Progress Celebration** is your time to reflect on all you've accomplished, identify any challenges, and keep your progress on track. Set aside 30 minutes to do a little "weed patrol" and celebrate your wins.

1. Weed Patrol

Take a moment to check in with yourself. **Are there any "weeds" (negative thoughts, self-doubt, or roadblocks) that have sprouted up this week?** Write down anything that has held you back or weighed on you.

Examples of weeds could be:
+ Doubts about your capabilities
+ Negative self-talk
+ Unanticipated obstacles

How will you "nip them in the bud" and keep moving forward? Describe a proactive step or mindset shift to tackle these weeds.

2. Action Review

Reflect on the actions you took during this past week. **Did these actions effectively nurture your Dream Seeds and target outcomes?**

+ What daily actions worked well in nurturing your goals?
+ Were there any actions that felt unproductive or off-track?

List a few adjustments you could make for next week to keep your actions aligned with your vision.

3. Initiative Check

Review the initiatives in your Watering Cans. **Are you on track to achieve each one?** Take a quick look at your key focus areas and consider any adjustments needed.

Which initiatives are moving along well?

Are there any that need a bit more attention or a different approach?

Note any tweaks or new strategies to strengthen your progress next week.

_____

_____

_____

_____

4. Celebrate Success!

Time to celebrate! **What successes or progress can you acknowledge this week?** Whether big or small, every step forward counts. Take a moment to recognize what you've accomplished, and feel proud of yourself for showing up.

- ♦ What are you most proud of this week?
- ♦ How can you reward yourself or simply honor your efforts?

Remember, progress isn't always about huge leaps—it's about steady, consistent steps forward. Give yourself credit for every victory.

_____

_____

_____

_____

3 Things/People I'm Grateful for Today and why you're grateful for them
ACTION STEP: If you've listed people here, send them a note to tell them.

1.

2.

3.

"To Do's" I'm Committing to Accomplish Today
ACTION STEP: Time block your to-do's in your calendar.

1.

2.

3.

What Am I Learning Today?	How Am I Serving Others Today?

How Am I Showing Up for Myself Today?

VISUALIZATION
Visualize the freedom your business brings, allowing you more family time. Picture yourself fully present with your loved ones. *Let this motivate you to build a life that honors both work and family.*

AFFIRMATION
Write at least one positive affirmation that resonates with you today and say it out loud.

DAILY DOSE OF AWESOME
My work gives me the freedom to enjoy time with my family.
Say this affirmation aloud at least seven times and use different inflection points each time.

JOURNAL

3 Things/People I'm Grateful for Today and why you're grateful for them
ACTION STEP: If you've listed people here, send them a note to tell them.

1.

2.

3.

"To Do's" I'm Committing to Accomplish Today
ACTION STEP: Time block your to-do's in your calendar.

1.

2.

3.

What Am I Learning Today?   ## How Am I Serving Others Today?

How Am I Showing Up for Myself Today?

VISUALIZATION
See yourself at the end of this 90-day journey, reflecting on how far you've come. Feel
the pride in every step you took. *Let this journey inspire you to keep pursuing your dreams
with courage and conviction.*

AFFIRMATION
Write at least one positive affirmation that
resonates with you today and say it out loud.

DAILY DOSE OF AWESOME
I am proud of the journey I've
taken and who I've become.
Say this affirmation aloud at least seven times and
use different inflection points each time.

JOURNAL

3 Things/People I'm Grateful for Today and why you're grateful for them
ACTION STEP: If you've listed people here, send them a note to tell them.

1.

2.

3.

"To Do's" I'm Committing to Accomplish Today
ACTION STEP: Time block your to-do's in your calendar.

1.

2.

3.

What Am I Learning Today?   ## How Am I Serving Others Today?

How Am I Showing Up for Myself Today?

VISUALIZATION
Picture yourself reaching a new level of financial security and fulfillment. Feel the peace and pride that come with stability. Embrace this as a reminder of your commitment to building something meaningful.

AFFIRMATION
Write at least one positive affirmation that resonates with you today and say it out loud.

DAILY DOSE OF AWESOME
I am financially secure and fulfilled by my work.
Say this affirmation aloud at least seven times and use different inflection points each time.

JOURNAL

3 Things/People I'm Grateful for Today and why you're grateful for them
ACTION STEP: If you've listed people here, send them a note to tell them.

1.

2.

3.

"To Do's" I'm Committing to Accomplish Today
ACTION STEP: Time block your to-do's in your calendar.

1.

2.

3.

What Am I Learning Today?

How Am I Serving Others Today?

How Am I Showing Up for Myself Today?

VISUALIZATION
Visualize a day where your business runs smoothly, even without you. Imagine the freedom to step away and know everything is under control. *Let this sense of ease inspire you to continue building a sustainable business.*

AFFIRMATION
Write at least one positive affirmation that resonates with you today and say it out loud.

DAILY DOSE OF AWESOME
My business thrives with ease, even when I step back.
Say this affirmation aloud at least seven times and use different inflection points each time.

JOURNAL

Feeling stuck about what to write about today and need some inspiration?
Scan this QR code:

3 Things/People I'm Grateful for Today and why you're grateful for them
ACTION STEP: If you've listed people here, send them a note to tell them.

1.

2.

3.

"To Do's" I'm Committing to Accomplish Today
ACTION STEP: Time block your to-do's in your calendar.

1.

2.

3.

What Am I Learning Today?   ## How Am I Serving Others Today?

How Am I Showing Up for Myself Today?

VISUALIZATION
See yourself going to bed tonight feeling peaceful and stress-free. Reflect on all you've balanced today. *Allow this peace to be a source of gratitude and strength.*

AFFIRMATION
Write at least one positive affirmation that resonates with you today and say it out loud.

DAILY DOSE OF AWESOME
I release stress and choose calm and clarity in every moment.
Say this affirmation aloud at least seven times and use different inflection points each time.

JOURNAL

3 Things/People I'm Grateful for Today and why you're grateful for them
ACTION STEP: If you've listed people here, send them a note to tell them.

1. ....

2. ....

3. ....

"To Do's" I'm Committing to Accomplish Today
ACTION STEP: Time block your to-do's in your calendar.

1. ....

2. ....

3. ....

What Am I Learning Today?	How Am I Serving Others Today?

How Am I Showing Up for Myself Today?

....

....

VISUALIZATION
Imagine having ample time for activities you love outside of work. Feel the joy of engaging in hobbies and self-care. *Embrace this as a reminder of the importance of nurturing yourself.*

AFFIRMATION
Write at least one positive affirmation that resonates with you today and say it out loud.

DAILY DOSE OF AWESOME
I make time for activities
that bring me joy.
Say this affirmation aloud at least seven times and use different inflection points each time.

JOURNAL

Feeling stuck about what to write about today and need some inspiration?
Scan this QR code:

3 Things/People I'm Grateful for Today and why you're grateful for them
ACTION STEP: If you've listed people here, send them a note to tell them.

1.

2.

3.

"To Do's" I'm Committing to Accomplish Today
ACTION STEP: Time block your to-do's in your calendar.

1.

2.

3.

What Am I Learning Today?

How Am I Serving Others Today?

How Am I Showing Up for Myself Today?

VISUALIZATION
Visualize yourself confidently turning down work that doesn't align with your values. Feel the empowerment of honoring your boundaries. *Let this guide you in creating a life that's truly fulfilling.*

AFFIRMATION
Write at least one positive affirmation that resonates with you today and say it out loud.

DAILY DOSE OF AWESOME
I honor my values by choosing work that aligns with my purpose.
Say this affirmation aloud at least seven times and use different inflection points each time.

JOURNAL

Feeling stuck about what to write about today and need some inspiration?
Scan this QR code:

WEEKLY PROGRESS CELEBRATION:
WEED PATROL & PROGRESS TRACKING

Congratulations on another week of growing your Dream Seeds! This **Weekly Progress Celebration** is your time to reflect on all you've accomplished, identify any challenges, and keep your progress on track. Set aside 30 minutes to do a little "weed patrol" and celebrate your wins.

1. Weed Patrol

Take a moment to check in with yourself. **Are there any "weeds" (negative thoughts, self-doubt, or roadblocks) that have sprouted up this week?** Write down anything that has held you back or weighed on you.

Examples of weeds could be:
+ Doubts about your capabilities
+ Negative self-talk
+ Unanticipated obstacles

How will you "nip them in the bud" and keep moving forward? Describe a proactive step or mindset shift to tackle these weeds.

_____

_____

_____

_____

2. Action Review

Reflect on the actions you took during this past week. **Did these actions effectively nurture your Dream Seeds and target outcomes?**

+ What daily actions worked well in nurturing your goals?
+ Were there any actions that felt unproductive or off-track?

List a few adjustments you could make for next week to keep your actions aligned with your vision.

_____

_____

_____

3. Initiative Check

Review the initiatives in your Watering Cans. **Are you on track to achieve each one?** Take a quick look at your key focus areas and consider any adjustments needed.

Which initiatives are moving along well?

Are there any that need a bit more attention or a different approach?

Note any tweaks or new strategies to strengthen your progress next week.

_____

_____

_____

_____

_____

4. Celebrate Success!

Time to celebrate! **What successes or progress can you acknowledge this week?** Whether big or small, every step forward counts. Take a moment to recognize what you've accomplished, and feel proud of yourself for showing up.

+ What are you most proud of this week?
+ How can you reward yourself or simply honor your efforts?

Remember, progress isn't always about huge leaps—it's about steady, consistent steps forward. Give yourself credit for every victory.

_____

_____

_____

_____

_____

3 Things/People I'm Grateful for Today and why you're grateful for them
ACTION STEP: If you've listed people here, send them a note to tell them.

1.

2.

3.

"To Do's" I'm Committing to Accomplish Today
ACTION STEP: Time block your to-do's in your calendar.

1.

2.

3.

What Am I Learning Today?	How Am I Serving Others Today?

How Am I Showing Up for Myself Today?

VISUALIZATION
Picture yourself accomplishing a long-standing task you've been putting off. Feel the satisfaction of clearing it off your list. *Embrace this as a reminder of the power of small steps toward big results.*

AFFIRMATION
Write at least one positive affirmation that resonates with you today and say it out loud.

DAILY DOSE OF AWESOME
I let go of all urges to procrastinate. Instead, I embrace focused action.
Say this affirmation aloud at least seven times and use different inflection points each time.

JOURNAL

Feeling stuck about what to write about today and need some inspiration?
Scan this QR code:

DAY 72   /   /

3 Things/People I'm Grateful for Today and why you're grateful for them
ACTION STEP: If you've listed people here, send them a note to tell them.

1.

2.

3.

"To Do's" I'm Committing to Accomplish Today
ACTION STEP: Time block your to-do's in your calendar.

1.

2.

3.

What Am I Learning Today?

How Am I Serving Others Today?

How Am I Showing Up for Myself Today?

VISUALIZATION
Imagine your personal brand growing and gaining recognition in your industry. Feel the pride and excitement of being seen as an authority. *Let this motivate you to continue showing up authentically.*

AFFIRMATION
Write at least one positive affirmation that resonates with you today and say it out loud.

DAILY DOSE OF AWESOME
I am building a respected, recognized brand in my field.
Say this affirmation aloud at least seven times and use different inflection points each time.

JOURNAL

Feeling stuck about what to write about today and need some inspiration? Scan this QR code:

3 Things/People I'm Grateful for Today and why you're grateful for them
ACTION STEP: If you've listed people here, send them a note to tell them.

1.

2.

3.

"To Do's" I'm Committing to Accomplish Today
ACTION STEP: Time block your to-do's in your calendar.

1.

2.

3.

What Am I Learning Today?

How Am I Serving Others Today?

How Am I Showing Up for Myself Today?

VISUALIZATION
See yourself supporting a fellow entrepreneur and feeling the strength of community. Feel the joy of lifting others up. *Embrace this connection as a reminder of the fulfillment you receive from helping others.*

AFFIRMATION
Write at least one positive affirmation that resonates with you today and say it out loud.

DAILY DOSE OF AWESOME
I support and uplift others
on their journeys.
Say this affirmation aloud at least seven times and use different inflection points each time.

JOURNAL

Feeling stuck about what to write about today and need some inspiration?
Scan this QR code:

3 Things/People I'm Grateful for Today and why you're grateful for them
ACTION STEP: If you've listed people here, send them a note to tell them.

1. ....

2. ....

3. ....

"To Do's" I'm Committing to Accomplish Today
ACTION STEP: Time block your to-do's in your calendar.

1. ....

2. ....

3. ....

What Am I Learning Today?

How Am I Serving Others Today?

How Am I Showing Up for Myself Today?

VISUALIZATION
Picture yourself achieving a target you once thought was beyond reach. Feel the thrill of surpassing your own expectations. *Let this experience empower you to set even bigger dreams.*

AFFIRMATION
Write at least one positive affirmation that resonates with you today and say it out loud.

DAILY DOSE OF AWESOME
I am capable of achieving
even my boldest dreams.
Say this affirmation aloud at least seven times and use different inflection points each time.

JOURNAL

Feeling stuck about what to write about today and need some inspiration?
Scan this QR code:

3 Things/People I'm Grateful for Today and why you're grateful for them
ACTION STEP: If you've listed people here, send them a note to tell them.

1.

2.

3.

"To Do's" I'm Committing to Accomplish Today
ACTION STEP: Time block your to-do's in your calendar.

1.

2.

3.

What Am I Learning Today? | How Am I Serving Others Today?

How Am I Showing Up for Myself Today?

VISUALIZATION
Visualize working in a beautiful, inspiring place today. Picture the joy and energy it brings to your work. *Embrace this as a reminder that your environment can fuel your success.*

AFFIRMATION
Write at least one positive affirmation that resonates with you today and say it out loud.

DAILY DOSE OF AWESOME
I create beautiful spaces that inspire my work and joy.
Say this affirmation aloud at least seven times and use different inflection points each time.

JOURNAL

3 Things/People I'm Grateful for Today and why you're grateful for them
ACTION STEP: If you've listed people here, send them a note to tell them.

1.

2.

3.

"To Do's" I'm Committing to Accomplish Today
ACTION STEP: Time block your to-do's in your calendar.

1.

2.

3.

What Am I Learning Today?

How Am I Serving Others Today?

How Am I Showing Up for Myself Today?

VISUALIZATION
Imagine a day where everything clicks—work, family, and personal time all harmonize. Feel the joy of balance. *Let this remind you that with intention, you can create a life that fits your vision.*

AFFIRMATION
Write at least one positive affirmation that resonates with you today and say it out loud.

DAILY DOSE OF AWESOME
I am in harmony, balancing work, family, and self-care.
Say this affirmation aloud at least seven times and use different inflection points each time.

JOURNAL

Feeling stuck about what to write about today and need some inspiration? Scan this QR code:

3 Things/People I'm Grateful for Today and why you're grateful for them
ACTION STEP: If you've listed people here, send them a note to tell them.

1.

2.

3.

"To Do's" I'm Committing to Accomplish Today
ACTION STEP: Time block your to-do's in your calendar.

1.

2.

3.

What Am I Learning Today?

How Am I Serving Others Today?

How Am I Showing Up for Myself Today?

VISUALIZATION
See yourself prioritizing self-care today without any guilt. Feel the empowerment of putting yourself first. *Allow this to become a regular part of your journey.*

AFFIRMATION
Write at least one positive affirmation that resonates with you today and say it out loud.

DAILY DOSE OF AWESOME
I prioritize my well-being, knowing that caring for myself strengthens every part of my life.
Say this affirmation aloud at least seven times and use different inflection points each time.

JOURNAL

Feeling stuck about what to write about today and need some inspiration?
Scan this QR code:

WEEKLY PROGRESS CELEBRATION:
WEED PATROL & PROGRESS TRACKING

Congratulations on another week of growing your Dream Seeds! This **Weekly Progress Celebration** is your time to reflect on all you've accomplished, identify any challenges, and keep your progress on track. Set aside 30 minutes to do a little "weed patrol" and celebrate your wins.

1. Weed Patrol

Take a moment to check in with yourself. **Are there any "weeds" (negative thoughts, self-doubt, or roadblocks) that have sprouted up this week?** Write down anything that has held you back or weighed on you.

Examples of weeds could be:
  + Doubts about your capabilities
  + Negative self-talk
  + Unanticipated obstacles

How will you "nip them in the bud" and keep moving forward? Describe a proactive step or mindset shift to tackle these weeds.

2. Action Review

Reflect on the actions you took during this past week. **Did these actions effectively nurture your Dream Seeds and target outcomes?**

  + What daily actions worked well in nurturing your goals?
  + Were there any actions that felt unproductive or off-track?

List a few adjustments you could make for next week to keep your actions aligned with your vision.

3. Initiative Check

Review the initiatives in your Watering Cans. **Are you on track to achieve each one?** Take a quick look at your key focus areas and consider any adjustments needed.

Which initiatives are moving along well?

Are there any that need a bit more attention or a different approach?

Note any tweaks or new strategies to strengthen your progress next week.

_____

_____

_____

_____

4. Celebrate Success!

Time to celebrate! **What successes or progress can you acknowledge this week?** Whether big or small, every step forward counts. Take a moment to recognize what you've accomplished, and feel proud of yourself for showing up.

+ What are you most proud of this week?

+ How can you reward yourself or simply honor your efforts?

Remember, progress isn't always about huge leaps—it's about steady, consistent steps forward. Give yourself credit for every victory.

_____

_____

_____

_____

3 Things/People I'm Grateful for Today and why you're grateful for them
ACTION STEP: If you've listed people here, send them a note to tell them.

1.

2.

3.

"To Do's" I'm Committing to Accomplish Today
ACTION STEP: Time block your to-do's in your calendar.

1.

2.

3.

What Am I Learning Today?	How Am I Serving Others Today?

How Am I Showing Up for Myself Today?

VISUALIZATION
Picture your inbox, calendar, and tasks organized and under control. Feel the relief and clarity that come from order. *Embrace this as a reminder of the power of structure and focus.*

AFFIRMATION
Write at least one positive affirmation that resonates with you today and say it out loud.

DAILY DOSE OF AWESOME
I stay organized, focused, and in control of my day.
Say this affirmation aloud at least seven times and use different inflection points each time.

JOURNAL

3 Things/People I'm Grateful for Today and why you're grateful for them
ACTION STEP: If you've listed people here, send them a note to tell them.

1.

2.

3.

"To Do's" I'm Committing to Accomplish Today
ACTION STEP: Time block your to-do's in your calendar.

1.

2.

3.

What Am I Learning Today?   ## How Am I Serving Others Today?

How Am I Showing Up for Myself Today?

VISUALIZATION

Visualize a loved one expressing pride in your journey. Feel the love and encouragement that come from their support. *Let this reminder strengthen your commitment to your goals.*

AFFIRMATION

Write at least one positive affirmation that resonates with you today and say it out loud.

DAILY DOSE OF AWESOME
I am surrounded by people who believe in me and lift me up.
Say this affirmation aloud at least seven times and use different inflection points each time.

JOURNAL

3 Things/People I'm Grateful for Today and why you're grateful for them
ACTION STEP: If you've listed people here, send them a note to tell them.

1.

2.

3.

"To Do's" I'm Committing to Accomplish Today
ACTION STEP: Time block your to-do's in your calendar.

1.

2.

3.

What Am I Learning Today?   ## How Am I Serving Others Today?

How Am I Showing Up for Myself Today?

VISUALIZATION
Imagine reaching a milestone in your business that allows for the lifestyle you desire. Feel the freedom and joy of achieving balance. *Embrace this vision as fuel to keep moving forward.*

AFFIRMATION
Write at least one positive affirmation that resonates with you today and say it out loud.

DAILY DOSE OF AWESOME
I live a life that honors both my work and my dreams.
Say this affirmation aloud at least seven times and use different inflection points each time.

JOURNAL

Feeling stuck about what to write about today and need some inspiration?
Scan this QR code:

3 Things/People I'm Grateful for Today and why you're grateful for them
ACTION STEP: If you've listed people here, send them a note to tell them.

1.

2.

3.

"To Do's" I'm Committing to Accomplish Today
ACTION STEP: Time block your to-do's in your calendar.

1.

2.

3.

What Am I Learning Today?	How Am I Serving Others Today?

How Am I Showing Up for Myself Today?

VISUALIZATION
See yourself handling a setback with resilience, turning it into a stepping stone. Feel
the strength that comes from overcoming
challenges. *Let this remind you of the growth
that comes with each obstacle.*

AFFIRMATION
Write at least one positive affirmation that
resonates with you today and say it out loud.

DAILY DOSE OF AWESOME
Every challenge is an opportunity
for growth and strength.
Say this affirmation aloud at least seven times and
use different inflection points each time.

JOURNAL

3 Things/People I'm Grateful for Today and why you're grateful for them
ACTION STEP: If you've listed people here, send them a note to tell them.

1.

2.

3.

"To Do's" I'm Committing to Accomplish Today
ACTION STEP: Time block your to-do's in your calendar.

1.

2.

3.

What Am I Learning Today?	How Am I Serving Others Today?

How Am I Showing Up for Myself Today?

VISUALIZATION
Picture celebrating a success with your team or clients, appreciating the journey together. Feel the unity and shared joy. *Embrace this as a reminder of the power of your community.*

AFFIRMATION
Write at least one positive affirmation that resonates with you today and say it out loud.

DAILY DOSE OF AWESOME
I celebrate my wins with gratitude and joy.
Say this affirmation aloud at least seven times and use different inflection points each time.

JOURNAL

3 Things/People I'm Grateful for Today and why you're grateful for them
ACTION STEP: If you've listed people here, send them a note to tell them.

1.

2.

3.

"To Do's" I'm Committing to Accomplish Today
ACTION STEP: Time block your to-do's in your calendar.

1.

2.

3.

What Am I Learning Today?

How Am I Serving Others Today?

How Am I Showing Up for Myself Today?

VISUALIZATION
Visualize a free evening spent with your family or indulging in a hobby you love. Feel the joy of quality time and fulfillment. *Let this motivate you to create space for joy in your life.*

AFFIRMATION
Write at least one positive affirmation that resonates with you today and say it out loud.

DAILY DOSE OF AWESOME
I prioritize quality time with loved ones.
Say this affirmation aloud at least seven times and use different inflection points each time.

JOURNAL

Feeling stuck about what to write about today and need some inspiration?
Scan this QR code:

3 Things/People I'm Grateful for Today and why you're grateful for them
ACTION STEP: If you've listed people here, send them a note to tell them.

1.

2.

3.

"To Do's" I'm Committing to Accomplish Today
ACTION STEP: Time block your to-do's in your calendar.

1.

2.

3.

What Am I Learning Today?	How Am I Serving Others Today?

How Am I Showing Up for Myself Today?

VISUALIZATION
Imagine a new opportunity arising from the reputation you've built. Feel the pride in knowing your work speaks for itself. *Embrace this as encouragement to keep showing up with excellence.*

AFFIRMATION
Write at least one positive affirmation that resonates with you today and say it out loud.

DAILY DOSE OF AWESOME
My reputation opens doors
to new opportunities.
Say this affirmation aloud at least seven times and use different inflection points each time.

JOURNAL

Feeling stuck about what to write about today and need some inspiration?
Scan this QR code:

WEEKLY PROGRESS CELEBRATION:
WEED PATROL & PROGRESS TRACKING

Congratulations on another week of growing your Dream Seeds! This **Weekly Progress Celebration** is your time to reflect on all you've accomplished, identify any challenges, and keep your progress on track. Set aside 30 minutes to do a little "weed patrol" and celebrate your wins.

1. Weed Patrol

Take a moment to check in with yourself. **Are there any "weeds" (negative thoughts, self-doubt, or roadblocks) that have sprouted up this week?** Write down anything that has held you back or weighed on you.

Examples of weeds could be:
+ Doubts about your capabilities
+ Negative self-talk
+ Unanticipated obstacles

How will you "nip them in the bud" and keep moving forward? Describe a proactive step or mindset shift to tackle these weeds.

2. Action Review

Reflect on the actions you took during this past week. **Did these actions effectively nurture your Dream Seeds and target outcomes?**

+ What daily actions worked well in nurturing your goals?
+ Were there any actions that felt unproductive or off-track?

List a few adjustments you could make for next week to keep your actions aligned with your vision.

3. Initiative Check

Review the initiatives in your Watering Cans. **Are you on track to achieve each one?** Take a quick look at your key focus areas and consider any adjustments needed.

Which initiatives are moving along well?

Are there any that need a bit more attention or a different approach?

Note any tweaks or new strategies to strengthen your progress next week.

---

4. Celebrate Success!

Time to celebrate! **What successes or progress can you acknowledge this week?** Whether big or small, every step forward counts. Take a moment to recognize what you've accomplished, and feel proud of yourself for showing up.

+ What are you most proud of this week?
+ How can you reward yourself or simply honor your efforts?

Remember, progress isn't always about huge leaps—it's about steady, consistent steps forward. Give yourself credit for every victory.

---

3 Things/People I'm Grateful for Today and why you're grateful for them

ACTION STEP: If you've listed people here, send them a note to tell them.

1.

2.

3.

"To Do's" I'm Committing to Accomplish Today

ACTION STEP: Time block your to-do's in your calendar.

1.

2.

3.

What Am I Learning Today?	How Am I Serving Others Today?

How Am I Showing Up for Myself Today?

VISUALIZATION

Picture yourself taking a well-deserved break, confident that your business will thrive in your absence. Feel the peace and freedom of true sustainability. *Let this motivate you to build a business that supports your life.*

DAILY DOSE OF AWESOME

I am free to take time off, knowing my business will thrive.

Say this affirmation aloud at least seven times and use different inflection points each time.

AFFIRMATION

Write at least one positive affirmation that resonates with you today and say it out loud.

JOURNAL

3 Things/People I'm Grateful for Today and why you're grateful for them
ACTION STEP: If you've listed people here, send them a note to tell them.

1.

2.

3.

"To Do's" I'm Committing to Accomplish Today
ACTION STEP: Time block your to-do's in your calendar.

1.

2.

3.

What Am I Learning Today?	How Am I Serving Others Today?

How Am I Showing Up for Myself Today?

VISUALIZATION
See yourself surrounded by supportive peers and mentors cheering you on. Feel the strength of being part of a powerful network. *Embrace this as a reminder of the importance of community and support.*

AFFIRMATION
Write at least one positive affirmation that resonates with you today and say it out loud.

DAILY DOSE OF AWESOME
I am surrounded by a powerful network of supportive people.
Say this affirmation aloud at least seven times and use different inflection points each time.

JOURNAL

3 Things/People I'm Grateful for Today and why you're grateful for them
ACTION STEP: If you've listed people here, send them a note to tell them.

1.

2.

3.

"To Do's" I'm Committing to Accomplish Today
ACTION STEP: Time block your to-do's in your calendar.

1.

2.

3.

What Am I Learning Today?   ## How Am I Serving Others Today?

How Am I Showing Up for Myself Today?

VISUALIZATION
Imagine fully stepping into your identity as a successful businesswoman, friend, daughter, spouse, and mom (pick all that apply!). Feel the pride and balance in embracing all that you are. *Let this vision guide you as you continue on your path.*

AFFIRMATION
Write at least one positive affirmation that resonates with you today and say it out loud.

DAILY DOSE OF AWESOME
I am a successful, empowered woman, bringing my best self to every role in my life.
Say this affirmation aloud at least seven times and use different inflection points each time.

JOURNAL

3 Things/People I'm Grateful for Today and why you're grateful for them
ACTION STEP: If you've listed people here, send them a note to tell them.

1.

2.

3.

"To Do's" I'm Committing to Accomplish Today
ACTION STEP: Time block your to-do's in your calendar.

1.

2.

3.

What Am I Learning Today?   ## How Am I Serving Others Today?

How Am I Showing Up for Myself Today?

VISUALIZATION

Picture yourself enjoying a day filled with things you love, feeling immense gratitude. Feel the happiness of being present and fulfilled. *Let this joy ground you in the richness of the life you're building.*

AFFIRMATION

Write at least one positive affirmation that resonates with you today and say it out loud.

DAILY DOSE OF AWESOME
I enjoy the present and find joy in the journey.
Say this affirmation aloud at least seven times and use different inflection points each time.

JOURNAL

3 Things/People I'm Grateful for Today and why you're grateful for them
ACTION STEP: If you've listed people here, send them a note to tell them.

1.
2.
3.

"To Do's" I'm Committing to Accomplish Today
ACTION STEP: Time block your to-do's in your calendar.

1.
2.
3.

What Am I Learning Today?

How Am I Serving Others Today?

How Am I Showing Up for Myself Today?

VISUALIZATION

Visualize your life and business flourishing, with all your Dream Seeds blooming. See yourself thriving in every area. *Embrace this as a reminder of what's possible with dedication and intention.*

AFFIRMATION

Write at least one positive affirmation that resonates with you today and say it out loud.

DAILY DOSE OF AWESOME
My life and business are flourishing and creating the impact I desire.
Say this affirmation aloud at least seven times and use different inflection points each time.

JOURNAL

3 Things/People I'm Grateful for Today and why you're grateful for them
ACTION STEP: If you've listed people here, send them a note to tell them.

1.

2.

3.

"To Do's" I'm Committing to Accomplish Today
ACTION STEP: Time block your to-do's in your calendar.

1.

2.

3.

What Am I Learning Today? | How Am I Serving Others Today?

How Am I Showing Up for Myself Today?

VISUALIZATION

Imagine finishing this 90-day journey with a heart full of pride, joy, and readiness for what's next. Reflect on all you've accomplished and who you've become. *Let this feeling of accomplishment inspire you to keep Living BIG.*

AFFIRMATION
Write at least one positive affirmation that resonates with you today and say it out loud.

DAILY DOSE OF AWESOME
I am proud of my journey,
ready to keep Living BIG!
Say this affirmation aloud at least seven times and use different inflection points each time.

JOURNAL

Feeling stuck about what to write about today and need some inspiration?
Scan this QR code:

DAY 90 | FINAL PRUNING

Congratulations on reaching Day 90! This final strategic pruning session will help you celebrate your progress, assess your journey, and plan for continued growth.

1. Growth Assessment

+ Reflect on your overall progress with each Dream Seed. Which seeds have grown and flourished?
+ What achievements or breakthroughs are you most proud of from the past 90 days?

2. Refinement

+ Have you gained any new insights that could guide your next 90 days? Are there specific areas where you'd like to focus more energy?
+ Are there any Dream Seeds or Watering Cans you'd like to refine or re-prioritize based on your experiences?

3. Course Correction

+ Look back on the challenges you encountered over the last 90 days. What major "weeds" did you overcome, and what strategies helped you succeed?
+ Are there any lessons learned that you want to carry forward? Outline any adjustments you plan to make as you set your next goals.

4. Nourishment Planning

+ Evaluate your mindset over the last 90 days. Have you grown in confidence, resilience, or balance?
+ Plan one or two key habits or activities to continue nurturing your mental well-being. Describe your vision for your mindset moving forward.

KEEP THE MOMENTUM GOING

Congratulations on Reaching Day 90!

You did it!

Take a moment to recognize just how far you've come. Over the past 90 days, you've shown up for yourself, nurtured your Dream Seeds, and taken steady, powerful steps toward the life and business you've envisioned. Every page you filled, every action you took, and every challenge you overcame has been an investment in *you*.

This is your journey, and you are truly making it your own. You're not just closer to your dreams—you're actively living them.

So, what's next?

Your momentum doesn't stop here. Every morning you wake up is an opportunity to grow, learn, and keep moving forward with the habits, clarity, and focus you've built. Imagine where you could be after the next 90 days, and then the next. With each cycle, you're strengthening the foundation of a life and business that align with your purpose.

Keep going, keep growing, and continue Living BIG. Let's make the next 90 days even more powerful, impactful, and fulfilling! Be sure to grab your next *90-Day Momentum Maker* at livebigwithstacey.com/momentum or scan the QR code.

Congratulations on your incredible journey. Here's to your ongoing success and to Living BIG—every single day.

Keep shining, and keep your momentum strong. The best is yet to come!

www.ingramcontent.com/pod-product-compliance
Lightning Source LLC
Chambersburg PA
CBHW071729120626
46550CB00002B/445